Kim Hyesoon

Tongueless Mother Tongue

Herausgegeben von
Matthias Kniep und
Katharina Schultens

Kim Hyesoon

혀 없는 모국어

Tongueless Mother Tongue

Ins Englische übertragen von Helen Cho

Ins Deutsche übertragen von Simone Kornappel

BERLINER REDE ZUR POESIE 2023

Wallstein Verlag

Die Berliner Rede zur Poesie wurde am 11. Juni 2023 im Rahmen des 24. poesiefestival berlin gehalten, veranstaltet vom Haus für Poesie.

Die Übersetzungen ins Englische und ins Deutsche wurden ermöglicht durch die Unterstützung des Koreanischen Kulturzentrums.

한국문화원
Koreanisches
Kulturzentrum

Inhalt

내가 출판사에 다니기 시작했을 때는 우리나라가 유신독재정권이 말기 증상을 보이고 있을 때였다. 그때는 인쇄하고 배포할 모든 신문과 단행본과 잡지에 대한 국가적 검열이 있었다. 그 때의 책은 활판 인쇄로 만들어졌었는데, 그 글자 한 자 한 자는 식자공과 문선공들이 다 따로 집자한 것이고, 편집부의 내가 교정을 본 것이었다. 그렇게 초교, 재교, 3교, O.K교까지 교정을 본 책을 가제본해서 시청에 가지고 가면 군인들이 군복을 입고 마치 출판사 사무실에서처럼 모여 앉아 시인, 소설가, 저자들의 원고를 검열했다. 그들은 출판할 수 없는 글자들이나 페이지 위에 검은 콜타르를 칠해서 돌려주었다. 그들은 활자는 한 자도 가지지 않았지만, 붉은 사인펜과 검은 콜타르 지우개는 보유한 출판사 위의 출판사, 인쇄소 위의 인쇄소였다. 글자가 지워지는 이유는 알 수 없었다. 우리나라에서 금지곡이 되었던 노래들처럼 그 이유는 검열하는 자들만 아는 것이었고, 글자를 지우는 그들의 핑계는 그 당시 우리나라에서 생산되던 책의 문장들보다 더 많이, 날마다 다양하게 생산되었다. 이를테면 건전하지 못하다든지, 군인을 희화화했다든지, 자유라는 단어를 썼다든지, 이 저자와 역자는 안 된다든지, 이 인용은 쓸 수 없다든지, 미풍양속을 헤친다든지, 이적행위라든지, 저자가 밤에 잠을 자지 않고 쓴 글이라서 안 된다든지, 아이들에게 나쁜 영향을 줄 거라든지, 밥맛이 없게 한다든지, 실패자의 타령이라든지, 등장인물이 싫다든지 하는 것 등등은 평범한 것에 속했다. 나는 검열이 끝난 책을 찾아서 돌아올 때는 울지 않았지만 저자를 찾아가 저자의 책이 콜타르칠이 된 저간의 사정을 얘기할 때는 울었다. 생애 마지막 저작을 출간하려던 경제학자 R을 찾아갔을 땐 죽음의 병상 머리말에서 저자의 죽음에 앞서 책의 죽음을 선언해야 했다. 그는 그 책의 출간을 보고 죽기를 바란다고, 부인이 대신 말해 주었다. 병상의 경제학자는 말없이 울기만 했다. 그의 길쭉하고 주름진 안경 속에서 눈물이 귀 뒤쪽으로 흘러내렸다. 편집자로서의 이런 경험은 나의 시 쓰기를 위축시키고, 내 시의 글자 수를 줄이며, 내 시의 리듬을 강팍하게 만들었고, 목소리의 변조를 실행하고 내 시를 위악적으로 만들었다. 시에서 나는 나의 직접적인 경험을 죽였다. 말을 빼앗기는 경험은 내 죽음에 앞서 혀가 먼저 죽는 경험이었다. 혀에서부터 온몸으로 죽음이 퍼지는 경험이었다. 말하는 순간 죽임을 당하겠지만, 그들은 말을 하지 못하게 해서도 죽였다.

나는 극장에서의 공연에 맞춰 출간하려는 희곡집 담당일 때도 있었는데 그 희곡은 제목부터 내용 전체가 그들이 칠한 콜타르 덩어리가 되었다. 왜냐하면 제목이 <개뿔>이었는데, '개는 뿔'이 없잖아?' 하던 젊은 군인의 목소리가 지금도 생생하게 들리는 것 같다. 개는 뿔이 없는데 그런 제목을 붙인 건 예술에 대한 모독이라며 그들은 그 책의 제목을 지웠다. 결국 작가의 이름과 출판사 이름만 덩그러니 남고 책의 내용은 모두 지워진 체, 숯덩이처럼 까매졌다. 나는 그 숯덩이 같은 책을 두 손에 받쳐 들고 작가의 사무실로 찾아갔다. 작가는 그 때 대중 운동을 하는 사무실에서 일하고 있었는데 직원 몇 명이 사회주의 국가 건설을 위해 비밀 서클을 만들었다는 죄목으로 투옥된 때라 경황이 없었다. 작가에게 원고가 사라진 숯덩이를 안겨 주었지만 그는 담담했다. 그렇지만 작가의 얼굴과 몸은 칼날처럼 벼려진 것 같았다. 작가 주위로 푸른 기운이 매섭게 서렸다. 이 시대와 이 나라를 저 사람은 저 칼날 같은 얼굴과 눈빛과 몸피로 지나가는구나 하고 나는 생각했다. 작가는 책을 못 내었으니 공연이라도 보러 오라고 했다. 희곡의 대사가 다 잘려 나갔는데 공연을 보러 오라니, 어떻게 공연을 한다는 말인가, 지하 비밀 공연인가? 나는 의아하게 생각했지만, 그는 시청 부

근의 유명한 연극 공연 극장인 세실극장으로 오라고 했다. 작가는 내 자리를 극장의 맨 앞줄 중앙 오른쪽에 마련하고 기다리고 있었다. 나는 공연을 관람했다. 그러나 그 연극엔 목소리가 없었다. 대사는 지워졌다. 배우들의 동작만이 있었을 뿐, 그 동작은 판토마임과 달리 아무것도 형상화하거나 과장하지 않았다. 다만 어떤 배우도 소리를 내지 않은 것뿐이었다. 어떤 배우는 긴 시간 무대 위에 서 있었고, 어떤 배우는 짧은 시간 무대 위에 서 있었다. 관객 누구도 그들이 그 무대 위에 서서 그들이 몇 달 동안 외웠던 대사를 어떻게 속으로 말하고 있는지 알지 못했다. 공연엔 몇 번의 구음이 무서운 비명처럼 쏟아졌다. 그 구음은 경찰서에서 심문받을 때 옆방에서 느닷없이 터져 나오는 소리 같기도 했다. 그리고 연이어 입안에서 웅얼거리는 비명을 씹어 삼키는 소리가 있었다. 배우들은 입을 벌리지 않았지만, 그 대사를 외웠던 시간이 신음이 되어 참지 못하고 폭발했다. 배우들에게 '몸짓만 하세요!' 라는 연출가의 지도가 있었겠지만 배우들이 그 동안 외웠던 대사를 참지 못하고 내지르는 폭발의 순간들이 있었다. 귀머거리의 외마디 소리처럼 터져나오는 폭발음들이 있었다. 살아 있는 목소리를 훼손당한 목소리유령이 내지르는 소리 같았다. 죽였는데도 죽지 않고, 언어의 세계의 문밖에서 목소리를 달라고 외치는 인간의 목소리, 언어를 빼앗김으로써 겪게 되는 이런 경험은 죽음이 먼저 죽은 혀를 거쳐 몸과 뒤섞이는 경험이었다. 배우들의 외마디 외침은 도살장에 도착한 어떤 다른 생물종의 목소리 같기도 했다. 이럴 때 침묵은 소리의 반대가 아니라 소리의 뒷면, 소리를 뒤집은 모습이었다. 물론 경찰의 감시 하의 공연이니 배우는 대사를 발설하는 대신 몸속으로 삼키고 또 삼켰다. 그들은 마치 태어나고 싶은데, 열리지 않는 자궁 문 앞에 웅크린 태아처럼 몸 밖의 엄마를 부르며 태중에서 문을 두드리고 있는 것 같았다. 그리고 이 언어 없는 언어를 가로지르는 한 목소리가 시종일관 나에게 들렸는데, 그것은 마치 모국어라는 것, 이 나라라는 것 자체를 애도하는 울음소리였다. 시청의 검열실에 앉은 자들의 핑계들을 애도함과 동시에 그들에게 언어를 빼앗긴 작가의 언어마저 애도하는 목소리. 희곡집의 교정을 본 나는 두 시간 내리 울면서, 입 속으로는 내가 교정을 본 대사를 웅얼거리면서 공연을 보았다. 아무 내용도 모르면서 관객들이 울었다. 작가는 조명실에서 공연을 보았고, 울고 있는 나를 내려다보았다. 얼마 후 그는 나와 가족이 되었다. 그 며칠 후 정보부장이 총을 쏴 대통령을 죽이는 사건이 일어나 대사 없는 연극 공연마저 금지되고 말았다.

시인은 자신의 유령(죽음)으로 쓴다. 시인은 자신의 존재를 자신이 존재하지 않는 부재의 무한에 투사해놓고 쓴다. 이 때 투사된 존재는 타자로서의 나, (시각적) 목소리로서의 나이다. 시의 유령은 작품이 시작될 때 작품을 이끌고 가는, 언어 이전의 목소리 안에 이미 숨어 있었다. 시의 유령은 우리가 이 모국어의 억압 속에서 혀를 빼앗기기 전, 목소리 안에 이미 있었다. 사라지고, 버려지고, 다치고, 죽어서 유랑하는 다른 유령(관객)들을 부르는 목소리. 아무것도 없어서 누구든 환대할 수 있는 목소리, 나 아닌 나를 부르는 목소리. 너 아닌 너를 부르는 목소리. 이 목소리는 언어 이전인 것. 언어학의 대상이 아닌 것. 심지어 소통과는 관계없는 것. 그 주파수는 너무 커서 오히려 들을 수 없는 것. 시인은 이 유령의 목소리로 언어의 세계를 헤엄쳐 나아간다. 들을 수 없는 사람이 나뭇잎 흔들리는 소리를 상상하는 것처럼 이 유령의 목소리로 언어 뒷면의 세계를 구축한다. 시인에게 자신을 부재하게 함으로써 생성된 유령이 없다면, 그 작품엔 영혼도 없다. 외설적으로 보일지도 모르겠지만 작품 속에 살아 있는 자신의 시체 없이는 살아 있는 시인의 목소리도 없다. 반대로 자신을 유령으로 만드는 그 목소리 없이는 작품도 없다. 시를 쓰는 자신의 목소리의 유령의 생성, 그것이 시다. 시인의 유령은 시인과 독자 사이에서 다시 출현한다. 작품을 읽는다는 건 이 목소리의 유령을 흡입하는 거다. 독자는 독서의 시간, 스스로의 목소리를 잃는다. 마치 독자는 어떤 '들림be possessed' 상태에 있게 된다. (한국어 '들림'은 듣다hearing, 들리다lifting, 들르

다stop by의 동음이의어다.) 목소리의 윤리는 유령의 발화 속에 있지 않고, 이 들림 상태 안에 있다. 들림의 번역에 있다. 역사의 잉여로서의 언어 속에 겨우 숨어 있는 유령에게는 언어를 몸에 묶지 않고도 외치는, 침묵, 한숨, 비명. 기침, 딸꾹질소리, 신음소리 같은 다른 목소리가 숨어 있다. 역사 쓰기에서 압살된 유령. 역사의 공백에서 우글거리는 유령, 여자들의 말 속에 숨은 유령. 시인은 유령을 채굴한다. 죽었으나 살아있는 것. 생기Das Eregnis, 그 자체이지만 소음이라서 우리가 일상에서는 듣지 못하는 것. 언어들 속에는 있는 듯 없는 것. 그러나 시로 구축하면 그 구축된 것 중앙에 텅 비어 있는 것. 시의 리듬을 통해 이 유령이 이행한다. 이 유령이 시인의 콧속을 투명한 쥐처럼 통과해 밖으로 나와 독자의 콧속에서 나온 투명한 쥐와 만난다. 번식한다. 사무치게 한다. 시인은 현실과 일상을 기록하는 척한다. 삶을 수집해서 늘어놓는 척한다. 하지만 시인은 유령의 목소리로 그것이 언어가 되어 나오는 발화 상태를 짓뭉개고 있는 거다. 그래서 시도 일종의 허구다. 이것은 지어낸 얘기를 쓴 것이 시라는 뜻이 아니라 시인과 독자 사이에 생겨난 장소가 일종의 허구라는 거다. 그 허구의 장소는 작품 속에서 시인이 그려낸 장소가 아니다. 그곳은 작품 밖의 장소로서 유령의 목소리가 독자와 만나는 다른 장소다, 그 장소를 허구의 거처라고 부를 수도 있겠다는 말이다. 그곳에 글자의 한계를 벗어난 시의 유령이 산다. 이 유령이 시의 바깥에서 독자에게 실재처럼 기능한다. 이 시의 바깥에서 유령의 목소리가 닿으면 독자에겐 세계 지도와는 다른 지도가 생겨난다. 이 장소에서 글자에 생기가 돌고, 이 글자에서 들려오는 목소리는 그 누구의 것도 아닌 시라는 시인의 유령의 목소리다. 리듬에 실린 언어다.

나는 <피어라 돼지>라는 시집을 발간하고 나서 어떤 지역 단체로부터 이 시집이 어떤 상을 수상하게 되었다는 전화를 받았다. 그 발표 후, 나는 그 지역 사람들을 '돼지'로 하대하는 사람, 혹은 모더니스트이기에 상을 줘서는 안 된다는 지적을 받기 시작했다. 나는 그 때 내가 모더니스트인 줄 처음 알게 되었다. 내가 수상하러 나타나면 나를 때리겠다는 사람도 있었다. 나는 SNS를 하는 친구의 도움으로 그런 글들을 전부 읽게 되었고, 그 즉시 그 수상을 사양했다. 이 시집은 일차적으로 구제역으로 몰살되는 돼지들을 다루고 있는 것처럼 보일 수도 있다. 그러나 나는 이 돼지들로부터 시작해 모든 살아 있는, 인간을 포함한 동물의 '몸'으로 시를 전개해 나갔다. 그리고 그 동안 우리가 다른 인간 타자의 몸을 포함한 우리의 몸을 어떻게 시선으로 체포하고, 어떻게 폭력으로 다루었는지를 반성했다. 나는 남해의 절에서 템플스테이에 참여하고 있었는데, 스님의 말씀이 가부좌한 우리들에게 떨어질 때마다 내 몸은 마치 선방에 앉아 있는 돼지 한 마리 같이 느껴졌다. 내 몸이 그렇게 비루하게 느껴질 수가 없었다. 나는 저 멀리 공중으로 떠올라서 내 몸을 내려다보았다. 돼지를 먹는 돼지의 몸을. 돼지로 다루어지는 몸을. 나는 육욕에 사무친 우리의 몸을 비하하는 스님의 말씀이 떨어질 때마다 그에 반하는, 혹은 핑계를 대는 시를 중얼거리는 나를 발견했다. 몸이 있다는 것은 '감각'을 갖추고 있다는 것이고, 고통을 느낀다는 것이다. 나는 그 때 침묵하는 돼지 행성의 돼지 한 마리로서 멀리서 돼지의 목을 자르고 희롱하고 마침내 먹는 지구의 나를 지켜보았다. 그리고 관점을 가진 인간인 나와 감각을 가진 동물인 돼지가 심지어 다른 행성에 있으면서도, 체화된 존재로, 같은 몸으로 있는 것을 보았다.

나는 <날개환상통 Phantom pain Wings>이라는 나의 시집에 '리듬의 얼굴 "이란 제법 긴 시를 실은 적이 있는데, 내가 그 시에 그런 제목을 붙인 것은 내가 그 시를 써나가는 중에 이글이글 타고 있으나 싸늘한, 사라졌으나 따가운, 버리고 싶어도 버려지지 않는 내 몸의 살아 있는 고통들, 그 고통의 리듬 끝에서 사라진 어머니의 희미한 얼굴을 보았기 때문이다. 내 몸의 고통은 고뇌와 달리 혀가 없는 리듬이었다. 그곳의 제일 깊은 곳엔 죽음도 넘어서는, 끝없이 '나'를 소멸로 밀어 넣는 리듬의 실체, 사라진 어머니가 있었다. 말하자면 내 고통의 주인은 언젠가 내 몸을 수태한, 내 몸의 주인이었으나 지금은 사라진 이의 얼굴로 거기 있었다. 내밀성으로 깊이 깊이 침잠해 가는 무한 수열의 그 고통. 그 리듬의 끝에 내 몸의 기관을 하나 하나 만들었으나 지금은 내 몸에 부재하는 어머니의 사라진 몸 같은 존재가 앉아 있는 걸 보았다고나 할까. 아마도 내 몸을 만드신 이는 자신의 몸의 리듬을 나누어 이 '나'를 만들었을 거다. 혀가 없는 리듬이 쓸개가 되고, 리듬이 허파가 되었을 거다. 그래서 나는 그 시의 제목을 '리듬의 얼굴'이라 했다. 나는 시는 결국 그 텅 빈 얼굴인 음악에 이르고자 하는, 그러나 끝끝내 종당엔 하나의 벌어진 입술 모양. 혀도 없이 발음되는 비명, 모음에 이르고자 하는 장르라고 생각한다. 엄마가 돌아가시기 전에 호스피스에 입원해 있었는데, 나는 엄마가 입원한 방에 들어갈 때마다 유리 믹서 속에 들어간 듯한 기분이 들었다. 엄마는 자신의 일생을 천천히 믹서로 갈아내고 있다는 생각이 들었다. 그 블랜딩의 리듬이 느껴졌다. 엄마가 경험한 산과 바다, 엄마의 시간, 엄마가 저장해 둔 공간들. 그리고 우리 형제들을 모두 소멸의 수학 속에 집어넣은 듯한 리듬 속에 있는 듯한 기분이 들었다. 그리고 엄마가 말을 하시지 못하게 된 날부터는 모음 한 개가 그 방안을 채웠다가 다른 모음 한 개가 그 방안을 다시 채우는 듯한 경험을 했다. 그 하나의 모음의 끝에 다다르는 수열이 리듬이라고 나는 생각했다. 루트 기호를 붙인 것처럼 하나의 숫자의 안으로, 안으로 들어가 마침내 모음 하나로 꺼지는 리듬 말이다. 거기에 이르기 위해 엄마의 리듬은 끝없이 헤엄쳐 온 것이었다.

나는 또 "맨홀인류"라는 긴 시도 쓴 적이 있는데, 그 시를 쓰면서 우리 인간들의 구멍은 하나로 연결되어 있다고 생각했다. 우리의 엉덩이는 하수구와 맨홀로, 코와 입은 바이러스로 가득 찬 공기로, 눈과 귀는 오염된 공기와 소음으로. 이 세상 사람들은 피부 껍데기의 색깔과 형상, 민족 등등에 따라 상하로 나뉘어져 있고, 좌우로 분리되어 있지만, 사실 우리 항문 아래 파이프는 하나로 연결되어 있지 않은가 생각했다. 호텔의 파이프와 쪽방촌의 파이프. 정신병원의 파이프와 성당의 파이프. 아시아인과 흑인의 엉덩이와 백인의 엉덩이. 그리하여 급기야 저는 우리의 신체 구멍들은 하나로 연결되어 있다고 생각하게 되었다. 어쨌든 우리는 얼굴 위와 발 아래로 같은 구멍을 열어 같은 파이프에 들이대고, 이 생을 영위해 가고 있다. 그것을 일종의 결핍의 연결성, 혹은 오물의 연결성이라고 부를 수도 있겠다. 우리가 죽음을 향해 함께 달려가고 있는 것도 같은 구멍을 향해 달려가는 것은 아닐까. 나의 '맨홀 인류'는 이 혀가 없는 구멍들과 파이프로 연결된 채 서로 평등하게 평등했다. 그리고 그 혀가 달리지 않은 구멍들과 파이프의 형태를 아우르는 우리의 거주, 과정, 흐름의 질서, 불균형 등등을 리듬이라고 부를 수도 있겠다고 생각했다.

시를 쓰다가 산문을 쓰면, 시로 돌아오기가 쉽지 않다. 왜냐하면 시의 필드에서는 시인과 대상과의 관계가 일대일이 아니라 다대다이기 때문에, 자신이 사용하는 언어가 당연한 일대일 세상으로 갔다가 돌아오려면 한꺼번에 이륙하는 여러 척의 우주선이 필요하기 때문이다. 시는 동일한 자아가 한 가지 정서와 논리를 가지고 진행하는 산문과 다르기 때문이다. 시는 어쩌면 글쓰기를 거부하는 장르인지도 모른다. 글쓰기에서 쫓겨난, 사람의 시간에서 쫓겨난 자가 쓰는 것. 그 거부된 자의 쓰기가 시이기 때문이다. 소설이 픽션만이 아니듯, 시는 암시만이 아니다. 시는 평론가와 숨바꼭질하는 장르가 아니다. 시는 목소리다. 아직 언어화되어본 적 없는 것, 언어화할 수 없는 것을 보이고, 들리게 하는 목소리다. 이 목소리 속에서 의미는 증발하고 없다. 언어를 습득하지 못한 사람처럼 개념이 형성되기 이전이다. 이 시가 도대체 무슨 의미인 거야? 네 이데올로기가 뭐야? 네 정체성이 뭐야? 하는 독자를 더욱 교란하려고 시는 써진다. 시에서는 시언어가 그 사물의 속성을 지칭하지 않는다. 사물은 한 언어로 말해질 수 없기 때문이다. 사물도 메아리로 말하고, 시인도 메아리로 말한다. 두 메아리가 만나 섞여든 목소리가 시의 언어다. 사물이 이식되어 확장된 몸으로서의 시인의 몸. 그러나 시는 한 인간의 인지 능력으로 사물 하나를 다 헤아릴 수가 없다고 생각한다. 사물 하나에 귀를 기울여 보라. 그 사물은 다성악처럼 여러 층위의 목소리를 낸다. 그래서 시는 일종의 무언의 대화이고, 다수가 웅얼거리고, 중얼거리고, 요동하는 일종의 소음이다. 이럴 때 시인은 분열적이고, 비합리적이고, 감응affect들인 목소리로 밖에는 그 '목소리'를 견디어낼 수 없다. 나는 그 중에서도 여러 번 내쫓김과 죽임의 세계를 거쳐 온 여성시는 자율적인 주체가 아니라 물질이며 신체인, 다양한 기관들의 응집체. 자신의 몸처럼 여러 기관들을 주렁주렁 매단 결집체, 그 기관의 유령들이 모두 중얼거리는 목소리라고 생각해 왔다. 이런 시를 읽는 독자는 자신의 자아의 장소에서 나아가 그 의미의 공백 속으로 들어가게 된다. 구멍 뚫린 문장 속으로 들어가게 된다. 피아노를 치면서 웅얼거리는 글렌 굴드의 중얼거림 같은 그 말의 공백 속으로 말이다. 사물도 삶도 시적 이미지가 되는 순간 원본의 이본(異本)이 되는 것처럼. 매일 매 순간이 이본들의 목소리가 들려온다. 그것을 가리키는 언어도 언어이면서 언어 안팎의 균열된 목소리가 된다. 부재로 탱탱한 중심을 때리는 북채가 된다.

우리나라에서 시 낭독이 끝나면 제일 많이 듣는 질문이 '너는 왜 시를 쓰나?'는 질문과 '이 시가 다 무슨 의미냐?' 하는 질문이다. 우리나라 사람들은 시를 들은 답답함을 직접적으로 드러낸다. 하지만 외국에서 시를 낭독한 다음 꼭 듣는 질문이 있다.'너의 시에선 왜 초현실주의가 보이는가', 이 질문에 이어서 자신의 한국문학에 대한 지식을 뽐내고 싶은 사람은 구체적으로 '너희 나라는 일본과 중국보다 초현실주의를 늦게 받아들였다고 알고 있는데, 너는 누구의 영향으로 초현실주의의 시를 쓰고 있느냐?'하는 질문이다. 이런 질문을 받을 때마다 나는 생각한다. 어찌하여 저 사람들은 낯선 것만 보면 초현실주의라 하는가. 미술엔 설치 작품도 있고, 미디어작품, 다양한 표현 매체와 방법론이 다 동원되어 있어도 그것을 모두 초현실주의라 하지 않는데, 시에 대해서는 왜 자신을

척도로 삼아 이해가 불가능하기만 하면 모두 다 초현실주의라 하는가. 표현 매체와 방법론이, 아니면 시가 발화되는 영토가 상이하다고 하지 않는가. 100년 전에 생겨난 그 'Sur'* 가 왜 아직도 신맛을 내고 있다는 말인가. 나에게는 시를 보는 눈을 키워주고, 시를 가르쳐 준 선생도 없고, 선배도 없고, 영향을 준 시인도 없었는데 초현실주의가 있었다고 외국 사람들이 나에게 가르쳐준다니 말이 되는가 하고 나는 생각한다. 그리고 이어서 저들이 일상적 언술로 읽기 편하게 쓴 것이 아니기만 하면, 낯설어 보이기만 하면 '초현실'이라는 용어를 붙이고, 우쭐해하는 건 아닐까 하고 의심한다. 요시카와 나기가 쓴 책 <경성의 다다, 동경의 다다>을 읽다가 1924년에 고한용이 경성(당시의 서울)에 도착하는 일본 다다이스트 쓰지준을 환영하기 위에, '다다이즘'이라고 쓴 깃발을 들고 서울역에 서 있었다는 대목에서, 나는 백 년 전의 어느 날 서울역을 떠올리면서 매우 크게 웃은 적이 있다. 거기 환영, 환송인파 중 다다이즘이 무엇인지 이해한 사람이 있었을까. 나도 누군가 나에게 영향을 준 초현실주의자 외국인이 있다면 초현실주의라고 쓴 깃발을 들고 인천국제공항에 나가 서 있으련만. 나는 그 질문에 이렇게 대답한다. 어떤 문학도 삶 자체는 아니라고. 문학은 본래적으로 섬뜩하고, 시** 고, 초현실적이라고. 그리고 우리나라엔 초현실주의라는 이름이 존재하지 않았을 뿐 초현실주의가 이미 있었다고. 그것은 신선소설, 유선사(遊仙詞) 등등의 이름으로 이미 씌어져 있었다고. 다만 너희들이 그런 흐름에 그런 이름을 지었던 것뿐이라고. 그래서 나의 시는 여기 지금, 이 문학판에 내 시의 장소를 둘 수 없으니 어떤 인칭도 어떤 시간 영역도 사라진 나만의 장소를 구축하고, 거기서 유령의 목소리를 내는 것이라고 대답한다. 그리고 허난설헌의 시를 예로 든다.

* 프랑스어 'sur' 는 '시큼한'의 뜻을 가지고 있다.

** 여기서는 동음이의어, '시'를 사용하여 시(詩)이고, 신 맛이라는 두 가지 뜻으로 사용함.

남편을 잃은 여자로 천년을 살다가
하늘 물가의 사람과 좋은 인연을 맺었다
공중에서 들려오는 밤의 음악소리는 지붕 끝에 매달린 달을 울린다
북쪽의 궁에 살던 여신이 발 앞에 내려온다
(-유선사 37)

허난설헌의 <유선사> 87편은 '이미' 초현실의 목소리다. 일종의 자기 최면이다. 여기는 '아니'라는 거다. 여기를 미리 애도한다는 거다. 남편이 버젓이 살아 있는 여자가 남편을 잃었다는 거다. 16세기의 어두운 골방에 앉아, 시를 쓸 때는 머리에 화관을 쓰고, 책상에 향합을 열어놓았다는 시인. 나도 머리에 화관을 쓰고 향을 피우고 시를 써볼까. 현실에서는 시를 발표하고, 자신의 시가 기거할 영토가 없으므로 저 공중과 현실의 중간지대에 자신을 보내놓은 27세에 죽은 여자시인의 모습. 시인은 현실에서는 가부장제의 볼모이고, 아들딸을 모두 잃은 슬픔의 볼모이지만 시의 세계에서는 외로운 신선으로서 자유를 구가하고자 했다. 그 중간지대에 목소리를 살게 하고자 했다. 허난설헌은 자신에게 세 가지 한이 있다고 기록했다 '이 나라에 태어난 것, 여자로 태어난 것, 결혼한 것'. 21세기에 사는 나의 세 가지 한과 이렇게 같을 수가 있다니. 슬픔과 고독과 내쳐짐과 학대를 한꺼번에 경험하는 16세기의 여자가 하루도 빠짐없이 자신의 방에서 비상한다. 그리고 이 땅이 아닌 달의 세계로 간다. 현실에서는 기거할 장소를 찾을 수 없으니, 저곳에 새 장소를 설치한다. '이 나라, 여자, 아내'가 '아님'의 장소를 온몸으로 횡단해 간다. 가면서 이미 죽은 자신의 몸에 유령의 목소리들을 가득 채운다. 타인과 공유할 수 없는 시체로서의 웅얼거리는 목소리들을. 우리는 이 목소리들을 눈으로 듣는다. 몸으로 듣는다. 이 목소리는 부권적 타자들이 강요한 영토에 대한 거부의 목소리다. 규범의 목소리에 대한 강렬한 저항의 목소리다. 27살이 되어서는 아무 병도 없던 사람이 목욕한 다음, 옷을 갈아입고, '금년은 3×9 수에 해당하는 해다. 오늘은 연꽃이 서리를 맞아서

붉은 색으로 변했다'하고는 눈을 감았다. 그리고는 다시 일어나지 않았다. 자신이 쓴 글을 다 불태우라는 유언을 남겼다. 시댁 사람들이 방안에 가득 찬 시들을 모두 태웠지만 동생인 허균에게 건너간 작품은 남아 중국에서 출간되었다. 몇 년 후, 우리나라의 진보 학자이며 소설가였던 박지원은 허난설헌 시에 대한 중국인의 칭찬에 대해 '일반적으로 규중 여인이 시를 읊는 것은 본래 아름다운 일이 아니다'라고 했다고 전해지고, 또 다른 진보 학자 홍대용은 '비록 이 부인의 시는 경지가 높지만 그의 덕행은 그의 시보다 멀리 뒤떨어진다' 했다고 전해진다. 16세기에 자유를 구가하던 멋진 남성 문필가들이었지만 여자가 조금의 자유를 갖기만 해도 죽이려고 달려들었다. 쩝쩝. 여자의 광기나 증후는 새로운 목소리의 나타남을 가능하게 하는 어떤 '다른' 상태일지도 모른다. 이 미친 듯 현실을 벗어난 목소리가 몸을 입으면 16세기 여자시인의 초현실이 된다. 허난설헌은 한자로 시를 썼다. 어쩌면 그녀에게 여자들이 쓰는, 여자에게 쓰라고 역설적으로 강요된 모국어(한글)는 그녀를 억압하고, 도덕 원칙을 강요하는, 견고한 체계였을 수도 있다. 모국과 모국어의 규범이라는 초자아에 대해서 그녀가 내미는 그 여자와 동성(同性)인 그 여자의 달나라. 그리고 그곳에서의 향유, 초자아와 전투를 벌이는 이 목소리의 발견이 허난설헌의 시다. 그 목소리는 여기 이 사람이 자신이 '아니라고', 이렇게 사는 것이 맞지 않다고, 이곳은 진짜 세상이 아니라고 그렇게 비명을 지른다.

나의 나라에 사는 모든 사람들이 부조리의 늪에 빠진 것 같은 나날들이 있었다. 슬픔의 성에서 곡하는 사람들이 쏟아져 나와 바람처럼 거리를 휩쓸던 울음의 나날이 있었다. 매일 흐린 날만 계속되는 나날이 있었다. 꿈속의 나마저도 검열의 불빛 아래 놓여지던 나날이 있었다. 나는 출판사의 보잘것없는 무색무취무명의 말단 편집사원이었다. 나는 누가 뺨을 갈기고 가도 아무도 알아채지 못하는. 왜 날마다 날씨가 흐린 것 같을까 이불 속에서 울먹거리는. 누구도 모르게 쓴 시들을 문예지에 투고한 편집사원이었다. 그 시절 한 형사는 나를 경찰서로 부른 다음 나의 출판사가 출간한 책의 번역자의 주소를 대라고 내 빰을 일곱 대 때렸다. 그가 나에게 쌍욕을 퍼부을 수 있도록 누가 자격을 준 건가? 나는 내가 뺨을 맞던 방을 핀셋으로 집어 올린다. 내가 검열받을 책을 들고 가던 방처럼 환한 그의 사무실. 내가 뺨을 맞아도 그 방의 누구도 관심이 없던 그 방. 모두 깜깜하게 불 끄고 숨죽였는데 그 방만 환하게 자주 나에게 떠올라 오는 방. 그 방에서 머리가 벗어지고, 흰 남방을 입은 큰 몸집의 남자가 두툼한 손으로 머리가 긴 나의 뺨을 갈겼다. 뒤로 물러나면 손을 뻗어 블라우스를 움켜잡고 당겨서 또 갈겼다. 그는 나의 '몰라요'에 대해 '이게 까불어? 이게 까불어?' 그리고 그 쌍욕들을 외쳤다. 나는 성냥곽보다 작은 그 사무실 상자에서 핀셋으로 자꾸만 나를 집어올린다. 그 다음 나를 삼킨다. 그러나 그것을 삼킨 내 목구멍에서 계속 웅얼거리는 목소리가 새어나왔다. 그 며칠 후 나는 출판사를 결근하면서 들릴 듯 말 듯한 목소리로 빰 한 대에 시 한 편씩. 시 7편을 썼다. 그 시들은 나의 시집 <어느 별의 지옥>에 실려 있다. 무서워서 몇 년이 지난 다음 시집에 실었다. 한 편은 전부 욕설로 되어 있어 시집에 넣지 않았다. 그 형사는 내가 다니는 출판사 담당이었는데 그 후에도 아무 일 없었던 것처럼 자주 나타났다. 편집장과 농담도 하고, 이야기도 하고. 나는 그가 나타나면 화장실에 가서 오래 머물렀다. 이야기의 사람은 이야기의 나라에 있다. 사람의 나라에서 이야기를 끄집어내면 그 줄이 너무 길어 내 몸을 다 감고도 너무 많이 남게 된다. 고백이 끝이 없는 고백을 자꾸만 불러오게 된다. 나는 붉은 줄을 몸에 칭칭 감은 나를 핀셋으로 끄집어낸 다음 그 남자와 내가 든 상자를 닫아서 밟아 버렸다. 그래서 내가 출판사에 다닌 시절 얘기를 짓밟아 버렸다. 목소리만 남기고서.

시를 가로지르는 목소리는 우리의 세계, 우리가 현실이라 믿고 있고, 현존한다고 착각하고 있는 이곳이 그림자의 세계라고 말하기 위해, 이곳의 균열에 거주하기 위해 다가온다. 시의 목소리는 이곳 바깥에 무슨 다른 장소가 있다고 말하는 게 아니라 이곳에 균열을 내면 부재의 세계가 보인다고, 우리에게는 '사이'라는 또 다른 세계가 있다고, 우리의 사이에는 벌어짐 그 자체가 현존하고 있다고, 그러니 이 현실 이미지들을 해체해 봐야 한다고, 비명을 지르며 다가온다. 그와 마찬가지로 시의 목소리는 각 단어마다에게도 큰 공백이 있다고 알려 준다. 그 공백 안은 코러스처럼 시끄럽다. 이 코러스의 웅성거림, 진동에는 물론 분명한 내용이 있지 않다. 그래서 시의 목소리에는 주인이 없다. 나는 주인 없고, 내용 없는 이 없음으로 없음을 향해 시를 써 나간다. 시의 목소리는 언어의 한 부분이 아니다. 몸의 한 부분도 아니다. 이 목소리에는 이름이 없다. 변증법적이지 않다. 목소리는 말해진 것이 아니라 들리는 것이다. 듣지 않으면 들리지 않는 것이다. 그저 울림이다. 비트다. 리듬 그 자체다. 시의 목소리는 줄거리가 아니다. 어떤 에피소드에 살을 입힌 것이 아니다. 안착할 장소도 없이 음악 속에, 심정 속에, 정서 속에, 변두리에 파편으로 살다가 불쑥 소리를 얻은 것. 그것이 드러나는 그 모습은 어떤 이미지, 어떤 에피소드라기보다는 인간의 언어를 몸에 두르지 않은 하나의 목소리일 뿐이다. 죽임을 당한 혀가 잃어버린 것들을 향해 가는 길목에, 혹은 혀가 추방되어 쫓겨나는 그 가장자리에서 어떤 목소리가 들린다. 시인은 이 목소리를 들을 때만 시인이다. 쓰는 사람과 듣는 사람 사이에서 단어의 공백들을 들을 때만 시인이다. 우리나라 사람들이 시인인 나에게 가장 많이 하는 질문, '왜 시를 쓰냐고?' 이게 다 무슨 뜻이냐고' 질문을 받으면 여기서는 도저히 살 수 없어서. 여기서 죽지 않고서는 도저히 살아갈 수 없어서. 유령이 된 내 목소리가 자꾸만 생성되는 유령을 구축한 것이라고 대답한다. 시는 죽음이라고, 죽음의 목소리는 여럿(複數)이라고, 그러다가 외국에서 너는 왜 초현실주의냐라는 질문을 받으면 제발 나를 초현실주의자라고만은 부르지 말아달라고 대답한다. 그러면 우리나라의 어느 시대의, 어느 성별의 시 대부분을 초현실이라고 불러야 한다고 나는 대답한다, 그리고 내 시라는 유령의 집은 목소리만 사는, 텅 빈 집이라고 대답한다. 그 구멍 같은 집에서 나의 시는 '시하고 있다고.' 나는 시로서 '당신하고' 있다고. 그 텅 빈 장소를 낙랑공주 (According to the Korean legend of the Princess of Nakrang, the royal princess tears apart the mystical drum that warns of foreign invasion to allow Prince Hodong of Goguryeo during the reign of Daemusin (A.D. 32) to invade the kingdom of Nakrang.) 처럼 큰 북채로 때리고 있다고, 왕인 아버지를 폐위시키는 위반의 대타자로서 여성적 향유를 제공하려 하고 있다고 대답한다. 내 목소리로 공기가 진동하고 울림이 퍼져 나간다고, 바람이 운다고 대답한다. 여성시인으로서의 내 목소리의 이행은 이런 모국어의 공백들 안에서 이루어지고, 내 여성적이고 시적인 욕망은 이렇게 모국어의 공백들 속에서 이행할 때, 비로소 내 한 편의 시를 펼친다고 대답한다.

Towards the end of the Yushin Constitution, I started working at a publishing house in Korea. During the last days of the dictatorial regime, all newspapers, books, and magazines were subject to government censorship. Back then, books were produced by means of type printing, whereby each letter was compiled by a type setter and a type picker before being passed onto the editorial department—for me to proofread several times. The galley proof was then taken to City Hall to be censored by soldiers in military uniforms. They gathered together as if inside a publisher's office, and scrutinized manuscripts written by poets, novelists, and other authors, scoring through words and passages that they deemed inappropriate using black coal tar. The censors were without a single type. However, with their red marker pens and black coal tar erasers, they became a publishing house above all publishing houses, and a printing house above all printing houses. I couldn't figure out the reason why some letters had to be deleted. As with the songs that were banned in Korea, only the censors knew why. Every day, they came up with excuses for scoring through words—excuses that were more diverse and copious than sentences printed in books. For example, some texts were judged to be unwholesome, and some books made a caricature of the military. The censors objected to the use of the word 'freedom', and vetoed certain authors, translators, or quotes. According to them, some publications offended public morals, or benefited the enemy. Some books could not see the light of the day because they'd been written at night, or because they would have a bad influence on children or decrease people's appetites. Other common reasons included the censors' aversion to the stories of failures or specific characters. My eyes remained dry as I picked up the censored manuscript and returned to the office, but I did shed tears later when I had to explain to the author the circumstances surrounding the censorship. Once I went to see economist R on a sickbed, who had been hoping to publish his swan song. At his bedside, I had to declare the death of his book before his own death. His wife said that he wanted to see the publication of his book before he died. The bedridden economist wept silently. Tears trickled down the back of his ears from his long, wrinkled glasses. Such moments I experienced as an editor put a damper on my poetry writing, reduced the number of letters in my poems, hardened my poetic rhythms, distorted my voice, and rendered my poetry dysphemistic. In poetry, I killed my direct experiences. The experience of being deprived of words meant that my tongue died prior to my own death. Death spread from the tongue to the rest of the body. The moment anyone dared to speak, they would've been killed. Yet, the censors also killed people by preventing them from speaking.

Every so often I was in charge of a collection of plays—scheduled to be published in time for a stage performance. One play ended up being blacked out from start to finish. It was titled *Gaebbul* (which literally translates to 'dog horn'). "But dogs don't have horns, right?" The voice of the young soldier still rings vividly in my ears. On grounds that such a nonsensical title was an insult to art, they initially blacked out the play's title. In the end, only the names of the playwright and the publisher remained. With the entire content of the play scored through, the play turned as black as a lump of charcoal. Holding the charcoal-like book in my hands, I made my way to the playwright's office. The man was engaged in the popular movement of the time. He was already in a predicament as several of his colleagues had been imprisoned for organizing a secret group aimed at establishing a socialist state. I handed him the lump of charcoal that had once been his manuscript. He remained calm, but his face and body looked as honed as a knife blade. A fierce blue aura hung about him. It occurred to me that he was passing through this era and this country with his sharp, bladelike face, eyes, and body. The publication of the book was thus scrapped, but he asked me to come and see the play in the theatre anyway. I grew curious as to how he was going stage the play when all the lines had been scored through. Was it destined to be some kind of clandestine underground performance? The playwright invited me to Cecil Theatre, a well-known venue located near City Hall. I watched the performance from the front row. The play was devoid of sound. The lines were gone, leaving only the actors' movements. Unlike in a pantomime, they did not embody or exaggerate anything. It was simply that none of the actors made a sound. Some actors were on stage for a long time, while some actors only made a brief appearance. Nobody in the audience discerned how the actors on stage silently delivered the lines that they'd practiced for months. Throughout the performance, several cries spurted out like terrible screams. It sounded as if someone were being interrogated by the police in the room next door. The actors chewed and swallowed one muffled scream after another. They kept their mouths closed. However, the hours they'd spent memorizing the lines turned into groans that exploded relentlessly. The director must've instructed them to 'gesticulate only', but there were moments of explosion when the actors couldn't help but blurt out their lines. The explosions burst out like the shrieks of a deaf person, or like the shouts of a voice ghost whose living voice had been mutilated. The voice of a man who does not die even after being killed, but cries for a voice, standing outside the door of the world. This extortion of language was akin to the experience of having death pass through the dead tongue first and then mix with the body. The actors' intermittent cries almost seemed to come from some other species arriving at the slaughterhouse. Silence was no longer the opposite of sound, but the other side of sound, or reversed sound. Performing under police surveillance, the actors kept swallowing their lines inside, instead of uttering them. Like fetuses waiting to be born yet curled up in front of tightly closed womb doors, they seemed to be knocking on the doors and calling for their mothers outside. The whole time, I heard a voice cutting across that language without language. It wept and mourned for the mother tongue and the country itself. The voice grieved for the excuses of the censors at City Hall. At the same time, it even grieved for the language of the author whose language had been wrested away. Having proofread the play's script before, I sat through the two-hour-long performance weeping and mumbling the lines I'd gone over. The rest of the audience, too, cried without understanding the play. The playwright watching the performance from the lighting room looked down at me as I sobbed. After some time, he and I became family. A few days later, the president was assassinated by the director of the Korean Central Intelligence Agency (KCIA). As a result, even the silent play came to be banned.

A poet writes with their ghost (death). A poet writes by projecting their existence onto the infinite absence of non-existence. The projected being is the otherized self, or the self as a (visual) voice. The ghost of poetry is already hidden in the voice that precedes language and leads the work at the start. The ghost of poetry is already within the voice before we are deprived of our tongues under the oppression of the mother tongue. A voice calling for other ghosts (audience)—dead and wandering after being vanished, abandoned and injured. A voice that has nothing and therefore welcomes all. A voice calling for 'I' that is not 'I'. A voice calling for 'you' that is not 'you'. This voice precedes language. It is not a subject of linguistic studies. It has nothing to do with communication. The frequency is too great to be heard. A poet swims through the world of language with this ghostly voice, which, like a deaf person imagining the sound of rustling leaves, builds a world on the other side of language. If a poet is devoid of a ghost created by their absence, then there will be no soul in their work. It may seem obscene, but without the poet's living corpse in the work, there will be no living voice of the poet. Conversely, there is no work without the voice that turns the self into a ghost. The creation of the ghost of the poetry-writing self's voice—that is poetry. The ghost of the poet reappears between the poet and the reader. Reading poetry is inhaling the ghost of this voice. The reader loses the time of reading—one's own voice. It is as if the reader is in the state of 'being possessed' (Note that the Korean word '*deulim*' ('being possessed') is a homonym for 'hearing', 'lifting' and 'stopping by'). The ethics of the voice lie not in the ghost's utterances, but in that state of 'being possessed' and in the translation of 'being possessed'. The ghost barely hiding in language as a surplus of history conceals other voices such as silence, sighs, screams, coughs, hiccoughs, and groans that do not tie language to the body. Ghosts that have been crushed in the writing of history. Ghosts swarming in the void of history. Ghosts hidden in the language of women. The poet mines ghosts. What is dead yet alive. What is vigor or Das Eregnis itself but cannot be heard in everyday life because it is noise. What seems to exist but does not exist within languages. What becomes empty in the center if constructed into poetry. The ghost fulfils it all through the rhythm of poetry. The ghost passes through the poet's nostril like a transparent mouse, comes outside, and encounters the transparent mouse that has come out of the reader's nostril. They breed. They give rise to poignancy. The poet pretends to record reality and daily life; the poet pretends to collect and lay out life. However, in the ghost's voice, the poet tramples on the speech that turns that very voice into language. Therefore, poetry is a kind of fiction. That is not to say that poetry contains fictional stories. Rather, the place arising between the poet and the reader is a kind of fiction. That fictional place is not what the poet depicts in the poem. It exists outside the poem as a different place for the ghost's voice to encounter the reader. In other words, that place can be called a fiction's abode. There lives the ghost of poetry that transcends the limitations of letters. Outside the poem, the ghost functions like an actuality to the reader. Upon reaching the ghost's voice outside the poem, the reader generates a map different from the world map. In that place, letters come alive, and the voice carried by each letter is none other than the voice of the ghost of the poet as poetry. It is a language conveyed in rhythm.

Following the publication of my poetry collection *I'm OK, I'm Pig!*, I received a call from a local organization about an award the book had won. After the announcement, some people argued that I should not be given the award because I had disparaged the people of the local community as 'pigs' or because I was a modernist. That's when I found out for the first time that I was a modernist. Some people even threatened to use violence if I should show up to receive the award. With the help of a friend clued up on social media, I read all those comments, and immediately declined the award. *I'm OK, I'm Pig!* may seem to deal primarily with pigs slaughtered in an outbreak of foot-and-mouth disease. However, taking those pigs as a starting point, I developed poetry as 'the body' of all living things including humans.

At the same time, I reflected on how our bodies—including the bodies of other humans—had been arrested by our gaze and treated with violence. I was staying at a Buddhist temple in Namhae, and every time the monk's words fell upon us sitting in the lotus position, my body felt like that of a pig inside a Zen room. My body had never felt more abject. I floated up into the air, and looked down at my body. The body of a pig eating a pig. I found myself muttering poems in opposition to, or as an excuse for the monk's words of reproach towards our bodies indulging in sensual appetites. Having a body means having 'senses' and feeling pain. As a pig on a silent swine planet watching from afar, I saw myself on earth decapitating pigs, ridiculing them, and then finally eating them. Pigs with the same senses as me—a human with a view point—existed as embodied beings in the same bodies even on a different planet.

My poetry collection *Phantom Pain Wings* includes a fairly long poem titled 'Face of Rhythm'. I gave that poem such a title because in the course of writing it, I saw the faint face of my mother that had disappeared at the end of the rhythm of pain—the living pain of my body that was ablaze yet cold, vanished yet sore, and undisposed against my will. Unlike anguish, my body's pain was a tongueless rhythm. In the deepest part of it, the reality of the rhythm transcending death and endlessly pushing 'me' into extinction—my absent mother—could be found. In other words, the owner of my pain was there with the face of the one who had once conceived my body and disappeared. That pain of infinite sequences sinking deeper and deeper into intimacy. At the end of that rhythm, the organs of my body were created one by one, but now I encountered an existence resembling the body of my absent mother sitting inside my body. Perhaps the maker of my body made this 'I' by dividing the rhythm of their own body. A tongueless rhythm must have turned into a gall bladder, and other rhythms into lungs. Therefore, I titled the poem 'Face of Rhythm'. I believe poetry is a genre that seeks to reach the music that is the empty face, the shape of the lips that open in the end, and screams and vowels pronounced without a tongue. My mother was in a hospice for some time before she passed away. Every time I visited her there, I felt as if I were entering a glass blender. I got the sense that my mother was slowly grinding her entire life in the blender, and I could feel the rhythm of the blending. The mountains and seas she'd experienced, her times, the spaces she'd saved. I felt as if I were inside the rhythm that put all her children into the math of extinction. The day she lost the ability to speak, a vowel filled up the room—followed by yet another vowel. To me, the sequence reaching the end of that single vowel was rhythm. The rhythm that goes inside a number as if having a root symbol attached to it, and then gets extinguished to become a vowel. My mother's rhythm had been swimming endlessly to reach that place.

I once wrote a long poem called "Manhole humanity". While writing that poem, I thought that all the holes of human beings were connected—our backsides with sewers and manholes, our noses and mouths with virus-filled air, and our eyes and ears with polluted air and noise. People in this world are divided vertically and separated sideways according to the color of their skin and ethnicity among other things. Yet, the pipes beneath our anuses are all connected as one. That includes pipes in hotel rooms, pipes in shanty houses, pipes in psychiatric hospitals, pipes in cathedrals, and backsides of Asian, black and white people. Eventually, I came to believe that our body orifices were all connected as one. After all, we open up the same holes on our faces and under our feet, and place them on the same pipes in order to go on living. It can be referred to as connectivity of deficiency, or connectivity of filth. As we run towards death together, perhaps we're running towards the same hole. My "manhole humanity" is equally equal with one another, connected by such tongueless holes. I thought that our habitation, order of the flow, and imbalance encompassing the shape of the tongueless holes and pipes could be described as rhythm.

If you write prose after writing poetry, it is not easy to return to poetry. In poetry, the relationship between the poet and the object is not one-to-one, but many-to-many, and therefore in order to travel to and from the one-to-one world where one's language is taken for granted, several spaceships must take off at the same time. This is because poetry is different from prose where the same ego proceeds with one emotion and logic. Perhaps poetry is a genre that rejects writing. Poetry is written by someone who has been ousted from writing and from human time. Poetry is the writing of the rejected one. Poetry is not simply about allusions, just as a novel is more than fiction. Poetry is not a genre that plays hide-and-seek with critics. Poetry is a voice. It is a voice that makes what has not yet been and cannot be verbalized visible and audible. Within this voice, meaning has evaporated and disappeared. This precedes the formation of concepts—like a person who has not acquired a language. Poetry is written to further disturb the reader, who asks "What does this poem mean? What is your ideology? What is your identity?" In poetry, the language of poetry does not refer to the attributes of the object. That's because objects cannot be spoken of in one language. Objects speak in echoes, and so do poets. The voice created by the two echoes mixing together is the language of poetry. The poet's body as an expanded body with objects transplanted into it. However, poetry believes that one person's cognitive ability cannot discern and convey one object in full. The object emits multiple layers of voices like polyvocal music. Indeed, poetry is a kind of silent conversation—a kind of noise whereby many mumble, mutter, and fluctuate. When this happens, the poet cannot endure that 'voice' except with a divisive, irrational voice of 'affect'. Above all, women's poetry, which has been expelled and killed several times, is not an autonomous subject, but an aggregate of various organs both material and physical, an amalgam of various organs, and the voice whereby the ghosts of those organs all whisper. The reader of this poetry steps out of the space of their ego and into a semantic void, thereby entering the perforated sentence. The reader goes into the empty space of the words that resemble the murmurings of Glenn Gould on the piano—just as objects and lives become different versions of the originals the moment they turn into poetic images. Every moment of every day, the voices of the different versions are heard, and the language referring to that is at once a language and a ruptured voice. It becomes a drumstick that strikes the firm center with absence.

When I give a poetry reading in Korea, people often ask me "Why do you write poetry" and "What do your poems mean?" Korean readers are forthcoming about their frustration after listening to poetry. However, in other parts of the world, I invariably get the question "Why does your poetry contain surrealism?" Those wishing to show off their knowledge of Korean literature ask a more specific question: "Compared to China and Japan, Korea was relatively late in embracing surrealism, so who influenced you to write surrealist poetry?" Such questions make me think, 'How come they label all unfamiliar things as surrealism? In art, there are installation works, media works, various expressions, media, and methodologies, but they are not seen as surrealism. Yet, when it comes to poetry, if people do not understand something using their own criteria, then they say it's surrealism, instead of perceiving the medium of expression, methodology, or the poetic territory to be different. How come that 'sur'[*] from 100 years ago still tastes sour?' It makes no sense to me that foreigners should tell me about surrealism in my poetry when I've had no teacher to nurture my appreciation of poetry, or poet to influence me. I suspect that they flatter themselves by attaching the word 'surreal' to anything they find unfamiliar or difficult to understand because it's not written in everyday language. Once, while reading Nagi Yoshikawa's *Dada in Gyeongseong, Dada in Tokyo*, I came across a passage about how Ko Hanyong stood outside Seoul Station in 1924 holding a flag with the word 'Dadaism' written on it to welcome Japanese Dadaist Jun Tsuji arriving in Gyeongseong (old name of Seoul). I thought about what Seoul Station must have been like a century ago, and laughed out loud. Among the crowd of people gathered at the station that day, who would've understood what Dadaism was? If I had been influenced by a foreign surrealist, I, too, would have waved a flag with the word 'surrealism' written on it at the Incheon International Airport. In answer to such questions, I explain that no literature is life itself. Literature is inherently eerie, poetic, sour[**], and surreal. Even before the term 'surrealism' was introduced, surrealism had already existed in Korea in the forms of *Sinseonsoseal* and *Yuseonsa*. That literary trend in Korea was later named surrealism. Therefore, since my poetry is not given a place in the literary world here and now, I build my own place in which grammatical person and temporal domains disappear, and then raise the voice of a ghost there. Here is an example from Heo Nanseolheon's poetry:

* French word for 'sour'.

** The homonymous Korean word 'si' is used to mean both 'poetic' and 'sour'.

After living a thousand years as a widowed woman
she tied the knot with a man from the sky's waters.
The music of the night from the air rings the moon
hanging from the roof's edge.
The goddess living in the northern palace descends
to her feet.
(Yuseonsa 37)

Heo Nanseolheon's *Yuseonsa* carries the voice of surrealism. It is a kind of self-hypnosis. It rejects and laments 'here' in advance. It says that a woman whose husband is still alive is widowed. The sixteenth-century poet sat in a dark room and wrote poetry with a corolla on her head and an open incense box on her desk. Perhaps I, too, should wear a corolla on my head and burn incense while writing poetry. The female poet died at the age of 27 after placing herself somewhere between the sky and reality because she'd found no territory for her poetry to dwell in. In reality, she was taken hostage by the patriarchal system and by the sorrow of losing her children. However, in the world of poetry, she sought to enjoy freedom as a lonely immortal, and keep her voice alive in the middle ground. Heo Nanseolheon wrote that she had three regrets: "I was born in this country. I was born a woman. I got married." Living in the twenty-first century, I have the same regrets. The sixteenth-century woman experiencing sadness, loneliness, abandonment, and mistreatment all at once soars from her room every single day. Then she departs from this land to go to the moon. Since she finds nowhere to live in reality, she sets up a new place there. She traverses with her entire body the place that is *not* 'this country, a woman and a wife'. Along the way, she fills her body that is already dead with voices of ghosts—mumbling voices from a corpse that cannot be shared with others. We hear these voices with our eyes. We hear them with our bodies. The voices reject the territory forced by paternalistic others. They vehemently resist the voice of norms. At the age of 27, the woman who had no illness took a bath, got changed, and claimed, "This year is equivalent to the result of 3 times 9. Today, frost has turned the lotus flowers red." She then closed her eyes and never got up again. Heo left behind a will that all of her works be burned, and a significant amount of her works were incinerated by her in-laws. However, her bother Heo Gyun kept several of her poems, and later published them in China. A few years later, progressive scholar and novelist Pak Jiwon said, "In general, it is not inherently beautiful for a woman to recite poetry" in response to the Chinese praise of Heo Nanseolheon's poetry. Another progressive scholar Hong Dae-yong commented, "Although she was an accomplished poet, her virtue lagged far behind her poetry." The great male writers who enjoyed freedom in the sixteenth century were ready to launch an attack on any woman who had the slightest freedom. A woman's insanity or symptoms may show 'another' state that enables the emergence of a new voice. When this insane voice that deviates from reality wears a body, it becomes the surrealism of a female poet in the sixteenth century. Heo wrote poetry in Chinese characters. Perhaps her mother tongue (*Hangeul*), which was used by women, and was paradoxically forced upon women, served as a rigid system that oppressed her and enforced a set of moral principles. The woman she represents with regards to the super ego linked to the norm of the motherland and mother tongue, and the woman's moon which is of the same sex. Heo's poetry conveys the enjoyment to be had there and the discovery of the voice battling the super ego. The voice screams that this person is 'not myself', this is not the right way to live, and this is not the real world.

There were days when everyone in Korea seemed to have fallen into a mire of absurdity. Mourners poured out from the castle of sorrow and wandered the streets like the wind. The weather remained cloudy day after day. Even in my dreams, I was placed under the glaring light of censorship. I was a member of an editorial team at a publishing house—colorless, odorless, nameless, and low on the totem pole. Even if someone slapped me, nobody would notice. I sobbed under my blanket, wondering why the weather seemed gloomy every day. I submitted my poems, which I'd written in secret, to literary magazines. One day, a detective summoned me to the police station, where he slapped me seven times, demanding the address of a certain translator. Who gave him the right to hurl abuses at me? With tweezers, I pick up the room where I was slapped. His office that was as bright as the room where I'd taken books to be censored. The room where nobody batted an eyelash even as I was getting slapped. In darkness and hushed silence, only that room—brightly lit—often floats up and comes to me. In that room, the burly bald man in a white shirt raised his thick hand and slapped me—I had long hair then. When I took a step back, he reached out, grabbed my blouse and slapped me again. When I said "I don't know," he shouted, "Are you messing with me? Are you messing me?" along with other swearwords. I keep picking myself up with tweezers from that office, which is smaller than a matchbox. Then I swallow myself. But then again, a mumbling voice escapes my throat. For a few days afterwards, I did not go into work. Instead, I wrote seven poems in a barely audible voice—one poem for each slap. Those poems are in my poetry collection *The Hell of That Star*. I was so frightened that it took me a few years to publish them. One of them consisting entirely of profanities was omitted from the poetry collection. The detective was in charge of the publishing house that I worked for, and frequently dropped by as if nothing had happened. He would joke with the chief editor, and share conversations. Whenever he showed up, I went to the bathroom and stayed there for a long time. People in a story are in the world of the story. When I extract a story from the human world, I find that the string is so long that I can wrap it around my body and still have a lot of it left. One confession leads to endless confessions. I pulled out my body with a red string tied around using tweezers, closed the box containing the man and myself, and trampled on it. That way, I trampled on the story of my days at the publishing house, leaving only a voice.

The voice traversing poetry approaches to tell us that our world, which we mistakenly believe to be real and existent, is merely a world of shadows, and to dwell in the crevice of that world. The voice of poetry does not claim that there is another place outside. Instead, it approaches, screaming that the crevice of this place shows a world of absence, that we have another world 'in between', and that since a gap exists between us, we must dismantle images of reality. In the same vein, the voice of poetry informs us that each word contains a huge gap, which is as noisy as a chorus. Indeed, the murmurings and echoes of the chorus have no clear content. Therefore, the voice of poetry has no master. In the absence of content and masters, I write poetry towards nothingness. The voice of poetry is not a part of language. Nor is it a part of the body. It has no name. It is not dialectical. The voice is not spoken but heard. It is not heard if you do not listen to it. It is merely an echo. A beat. It is rhythm itself. The voice of poetry is not a plot. It does not flesh out an episode. It is something that suddenly gains sound after living as a fragment on the periphery—in the music, in the heart, in the emotions without a place to settle down. What is revealed is not an image or an episode but a voice unfettered by human language. A voice can be heard on the path of a slain tongue towards lost things, or on the edge of the tongue's exile. A poet is a poet only when they hear this voice—only when they hear the gaps in words between the writer and the listener. When Korean readers ask me "Why do you write poetry? What does it all mean?", I answer that because I can't live here without dying, my voice that has become a ghost has constructed a ghost that continues to come into being. I explain that poetry is death, and that the voice of death is plural. Then, when people outside of Korea question why I'm a surrealist, I ask them not to call me that because it would mean most of the poems written in a certain era and of a certain gender should be described as surrealist, too. I answer that the haunted house of my poetry is but an empty house occupied by a voice only. In that hole-like house, my poetry 'does poetry', and through poetry, I 'do you'. I tell them that I beat that empty space with a large drumstick like the Princess of Nakrang (According to the Korean legend of the Princess of Nakrang, the royal princess tears apart the mystical drum that warns of foreign invasion to allow Prince Hodong of Goguryeo during the reign of Daemusin (A.D. 32) to invade the kingdom of Nakrang.) and strive to offer feminine enjoyment as the other of violation that dethrones the father. I answer that the air vibrates and resonates with my voice, and the wind cries. The implementation of my voice as a female poet takes place in the voids of the mother tongue. When my feminine and poetic desires are fulfilled in the voids of the mother tongue, I can finally unravel a poem.

Als sich die Präsidentenrepublik Koreas* ihrem Ende näherte, begann ich in einem koreanischen Verlagshaus zu arbeiten. Das diktatorische Regime unterwarf alle Zeitungen, alle Bücher und Zeitschriften der staatlichen Zensur. Bücher produzierte man damals im typographischen Schriftsatz, jeder Buchstabe wurde von Hand- und Schriftsetzern her- und zusammengestellt, bevor der Text an das Lektorat weiterging und ich ihn in vier Korrekturgängen las. Die Druckfahne wurde dann ins Rathaus gebracht, wo sie von uniformierten Soldaten zensiert wurde. Sie versammelten sich wie in einem Verlagsbüro und unterzogen die Manuskripte von Dichtern:innen, Romanautor:innen und anderen Schriftsteller:innnen einer genauen Prüfung, schwärzten Wörter und Passagen, die sie für unpassend hielten, mit Kohlenteer. Die Zensoren hatten keine eigenen Typen. Doch mit ihren roten Filzstiften und schwarzen Kohleteerradierern wurden sie zu einem Verlag über allen Verlagen, zu einer Druckerei über allen Druckereien. Mir blieb der Grund verborgen, warum einige Wörter gestrichen wurden. Wie bei Liedern, die in Korea verboten waren, wussten nur die Zensoren, warum. Jeden Tag ließen sie sich Ausreden für die Streichungen einfallen. Ausreden, die vielfältiger und umfangreicher waren als die in Büchern abgedruckten Sätze. So wurden beispielsweise einige Texte schlicht als ungesund eingestuft, von einigen Büchern hieß es, sie karikierten das Militär. Die Zensoren beanstandeten die Verwendung des Wortes ›Freiheit‹ und

* 유신 Yushin-Verfassung, Restauration, achte Verfassung Südkoreas

legten gegen bestimmte Autor:innen, Übersetzer:innen oder Zitate Widerspruch ein. Sie waren der Meinung, dass einige Publikationen gegen die öffentliche Moral verstießen oder dem Feind zugutekämen. Einige Bücher durften nicht erscheinen, weil sie angeblich von Autor:innen stammten, die nachts nicht schliefen, oder weil sie einen schlechten Einfluss auf Kinder hätten oder den Appetit der Menschen verderben würden. Zu den anderen üblichen Gründen zählte die Abneigung der Zensoren gegen Geschichten über Verlierer oder sonstige eigentümliche Charaktere. Meine Augen blieben trocken, als ich mit dem zensierten Manuskript ins Büro zurückkehrte, weinen musste ich erst, als ich dem Autor die Umstände der Zensur erklären musste. Einmal besuchte ich den Ökonomen R., der auf dem Krankenbett lag und seinen Schwanengesang zu veröffentlichen hoffte. An seinem Krankenbett musste ich den Tod seines Buches vor seinem eigenen Tod verkünden. Seine Frau sagte, er wolle, dass sein Buch noch vor seinem Tode veröffentlicht wird. Der bettlägerige Ökonom weinte leise. Von seiner großen, verbogenen Brille rannen die Tränen an seinen Ohren herunter. Solche Momente, die ich als Lektorin erlebte, hemmten mein Schreiben, reduzierten die Anzahl der Wörter in meinen Gedichten, gaben mir einen widerspenstigen poetischen Rhythmus, verzerrten meine Stimme und machten meine Gedichte anfällig für einen Dysphemismus. In der Poesie tötete ich meine unmittelbaren Erfahrungen. Die Erfahrung, der eigenen Worte beraubt zu werden, bedeutete, dass meine Zunge noch vor mir starb. Der Tod breitete sich von der Zunge auf den Rest des Körpers aus. In dem Moment, in dem jemand es gewagt hätte, zu sprechen, wäre er getötet worden. Auch die Zensoren töteten Menschen, indem sie sie am Sprechen hinderten.

Hin und wieder war ich für eine Sammlung von Theaterstücken verantwortlich, die rechtzeitig vor einer Aufführrung veröffentlicht werden sollten. Ein Stück war schließlich durch und durch geschwärzt – wie ein Klumpen Kohlenteer. Es trug den Titel *Gaebbul* (was wörtlich übersetzt »Hundehorn« bedeutet). »Aber Hunde haben doch keine Hörner, nicht wahr?« Die Stimme des jungen Soldaten klingt mir noch in den Ohren. Mit der Begründung, dass ein so unsinniger Titel eine Beleidigung der Kunst sei, wurde zunächst der Titel des Stücks geschwärzt. Am Ende blieben nur noch die Namen des Autors und des Verlegers übrig. Da der gesamte Inhalt durchgestrichen wurde, war das Stück schwarz wie ein Stück Kohle. Das »verkohlte« Buch behutsam in Händen tragend, begab ich mich ins Büro des Dramatikers. Damals war er in der Volksbewegung engagiert. Er befand sich bereits in einer misslichen Lage, da mehrere seiner Kollegen wegen der Organisation einer geheimen Gruppe zur Errichtung eines sozialistischen Staates inhaftiert worden waren. Ich reichte ihm den Klumpen Kohle, der einmal sein Manuskript gewesen war. Er blieb ruhig, Gesicht und Körper aber wirkten geschliffen wie eine Messerklinge. Es umgab ihn eine stechende blaue Aura. Und ich stellte mir vor, wie er Zeit und Land durchlief mit seinem spitzen, messerscharfen Gesicht, seinem Blick und Körper. Die Veröffentlichung des Buches wurde verworfen, er aber bat mich, das Stück trotzdem im Theater anzusehen. Ich war neugierig darauf, wie er das Stück inszenieren würde, wenn doch alle Zeilen durchgestrichen waren. Sollte es eine Art geheime Untergrundaufführung werden? Der Dramatiker lud mich ins Cecil Theater ein, einem bekannten Spielort in der Nähe des Rathauses. Ich verfolgte die Aufführung von der ersten Reihe aus. Das Stück war ohne Ton. Da war kein Text mehr, nur noch die Bewegungen der Schauspieler. Anders als bei einer Pantomime wurde nichts verkörpert oder übertrieben dargestellt. Es war einfach so, dass keine:r der Schauspieler:innen einen Ton von sich gab. Einige von ihnen befanden sich längere

Zeit auf der Bühne, andere nur kurz. Niemand im Publikum konnte genau erkennen, wie die Schauspieler:innen auf der Bühne den Text, den sie stundenlang geübt hatten, stumm vortrugen.

Während der Aufführung gab es mehrmals Rufe, die wie schreckliche Schreie klangen. Es hörte sich so an, als würde jemand im Nebenraum von der Polizei verhört. Die Schauspieler:innen kauten und schluckten einen gedämpften Schrei nach dem anderen herunter. Sie hielten ihre Münder geschlossen. Doch die Monate, die sie mit dem Auswendiglernen des Textes verbracht hatten, verwandelten sich in ein Stöhnen, das unerbittlich ausbrach. Der Regisseur musste ihnen die Anweisung »nur gestikulieren« gegeben haben, aber es gab Momente der Explosion, in denen die Schauspieler:innen nicht anders konnten, und der Text brach aus ihnen heraus. Diese Explosionen klangen wie die Schreie eines Gehörlosen oder wie die Rufe eines Gespenstes, dessen lebendige Stimme verstümmelt worden war. Die Stimme eines Menschen, der nicht stirbt, selbst wenn er getötet wird, sondern nach einer Stimme außerhalb der sprachlichen Welt schreit. Dieses Erlöschen der Sprache glich der Erfahrung des Todes, welcher zunächst die Zunge erreicht und sich erst dann mit dem Körper vermischt. Die vereinzelten Schreie der Schauspieler:innen schienen fast von einer anderen Spezies zu stammen, einer, die zum Schlachthof gebracht wird. Und die Stille war nicht mehr das Gegenteil des Klangs, sondern dessen Rückseite, der umgekehrte Klang. Unter Polizeiüberwachung schluckten die Schauspieler:innen ihren Text in sich hinein, anstatt ihn auszusprechen. Wie Föten, die auf ihre Geburt warten und vor fest verschlossenen Gebärmuttertüren kauern, schienen sie von innen an diese Türen zu klopfen und nach ihren Müttern draußen zu rufen. Und durch diese Sprache ohne Sprache hindurch hörte ich immer wieder eine Stimme. Sie weinte und trauerte um die Muttersprache und das Land selbst. Die Stimme war bekümmert über die Ausreden der Zensoren im Rathaus. Gleichzeitig trauerte sie um die Sprache des Autors, der seiner Sprache beraubt worden war. Da ich das Skript des Stücks zuvor Korrektur gelesen hatte, saß ich während der zweistündigen Aufführung weinend da, sprach murmelnd die Zeilen mit, die ich durchgesehen hatte. Auch der Rest des Publikums weinte, ohne das Stück zu verstehen. Der Dramatiker, der die Aufführung vom Beleuchtungsraum aus verfolgte, blickte zu mir herunter, während ich schluchzte. Bald darauf wurden er und ich eine Familie. Einige Tage darauf wurde der Präsident vom Direktor des koreanischen Geheimdienstes (KCIA) ermordet. Als Folge davon verbot man sogar das stumme Theaterstück.

Ein:e Dichter:in schreibt mit ihrem Geist (Tod). Ein:e Dichter:in schreibt, indem sie ihre Existenz auf die unendliche Abwesenheit der Nicht-Existenz projiziert. Das projizierte Wesen ist das verfremdete Selbst oder das Selbst als (visuelle) Stimme. Das Gespenst der Poesie ist bereits in der Stimme verborgen, die der Sprache vorausgeht und das Werk zu Beginn leitet. Das Gespenst der Poesie befindet sich schon in der Stimme, bevor wir durch Unterdrückung der Muttersprache unserer Zungen beraubt werden. Eine Stimme, die nach anderen Gespenstern (Zuhörer:innen) ruft, die tot sind und umherwandern, die entschwanden, verlassen wurden und verletzt. Eine Stimme, die nichts besitzt und deshalb jeden willkommen heißt. Eine Stimme, die nach dem »Ich« ruft, das nicht »Ich« ist. Eine Stimme, die nach dem »Du« ruft, das nicht »Du« ist. Diese Stimme geht der Sprache voraus. Sie ist nicht Gegenstand linguistischer Studien. Sie hat nichts mit Kommunikation zu tun. Die Frequenz ist zu hoch, um gehört zu werden. Ein:e Dichter:in schwimmt durch die Welt der Sprache mit dieser Gespenster-Stimme, die sich, gleich einem gehörlosen Menschen, der sich das Rascheln von Blättern nur vorstellt, eine Welt hinter der Sprache erschafft. Wenn Dichter:innen kein Gespenst besitzen, das durch ihre Abwesenheit entsteht, dann besitzt auch ihr Werk keine Seele. Es mag obszön erscheinen, aber es gibt keine lebendige Stimme der Dichter:innen ohne einen lebenden Leichnam im Werk. Umgekehrt gibt es kein Werk ohne eine Stimme, die das Selbst in ein Gespenst verwandelt. Das Gespenst der eigenen Stimme erschaffen, das dichtende Ich – das ist Poesie. Das Gespenst der Dichter:innen taucht zwischen den Dichter:innen und den Leser:innen wieder auf. Das Lesen von Gedichten ist das Einatmen dieser Stimmengespenster. Die Leser:innen verlieren die Zeit der Lektüre – die eigene Stimme. Es ist, als befände sich der Lesende im Zustand des »Besessenseins« (man beachte, dass das koreanische Wort ›deulim‹ (›besessen sein‹) tatsächlich ein Homonym für ›hören‹, ›aufheben‹ und ›vorbeischauen‹ ist). Die Ethik der Stimme liegt nicht in den Äußerungen des Geistes, sondern in diesem Zustand des »Besessenseins« und in der Übersetzung dieses »Besessenseins«. Das Gespenst, das sich gerade noch in der Sprache versteckt, verbirgt als Überschuss der Geschichte andere Stimmen, verbirgt Schweigen, Seufzen, Schreien, Husten, Schluckauf und Stöhnen, die die Sprache nicht an den Körper binden. Gespenster, die in der Geschichtsschreibung unterdrückt wurden, Gespenster, die herumschwirren in der Leere der Geschichte. Gespenster, die in der Sprache von Frauen verborgen sind. Die Dichter:innen schürfen nach Gespenstern. Was tot und doch lebendig ist. Was Lebenskraft oder das Ereignis selbst ist, aber im Alltag nicht gehört werden kann, schlicht weil es Lärm ist. Was zu existieren scheint, aber in den Sprachen nicht existiert. Was leer im Zentrum liegt, wenn es in der Poesie erschaffen wird. Das Gespenst erfüllt alles durch den Rhythmus der Poesie. Das Gespenst schlüpft durch das Nasenloch der Dichter:innen wie eine durchsichtige Maus, dringt nach außen und trifft auf jene andere durchsichtige Maus, die aus dem Nasenloch der Leser:innen schlüpfte. Sie pflanzen sich miteinander fort. Sie geben Anlass zur Schärfe. Die Dichter:innen geben vor, die Wirklichkeit und das alltägliche Leben aufzuzeichnen; die Dichter:innen geben vor, das Leben zu sammeln und zu entwerfen. Doch durch die Stimme des Geistes treten die Dichter:innen die Sprache mit Füßen, die eben diese Stimme in Sprache verwandelt. Die Poesie ist daher eine Art Fiktion. Das heißt jedoch nicht, dass die Poesie erfundene Geschichten enthält. Vielmehr ist jener Ort, der zwischen den Dichter:innen und Leser:innen entsteht, eine Art Fiktion. Dieser fiktionale Ort ist nicht das, was die Dichter:innen im Gedicht darstellen. Er existiert außerhalb des Gedichts als ein anderer Ort, an dem das Stimmengespenst dem Lesenden begegnet. Mit anderen Worten: Dieser Ort kann als Wohnstätte der Fiktion bezeichnet werden. Dort lebt das Gespenst der Poesie, das die Grenzen der Worte überschreitet. Außerhalb des Gedichts erscheint das Gespenst für die Leser:innen real. Wenn sie die Stimme des Gespenstes außerhalb des Gedichts erreicht, entsteht eine Karte, die sich von der Weltkarte unterscheidet. An diesem Ort werden die Wörter lebendig, und die Stimme, die von jedem Wort getragen wird, ist nichts anderes als die Stimme des Gespenstes der Dichter:innen in Form von Poesie. Es ist eine Sprache, die sich über den Rhythmus mitteilt.

Nach der Veröffentlichung meines Gedichtbandes *Blühe, Schwein, Blühe!* erhielt ich einen Anruf einer lokalen Organisation aufgrund einer Auszeichnung, die das Buch erhalten hatte. Nach der Bekanntgabe argumentierten einige Leute, dass ich den Preis nicht bekommen sollte, weil ich die Menschen in der lokalen Gemeinschaft als »Schweine« verunglimpft hätte oder weil ich eine Modernistin sei. Hier erfuhr ich zum ersten Mal, dass ich das war, eine

Modernistin. Einige Leute drohten mir sogar mit Gewalt, falls ich zur Preisverleihung erscheinen sollte. Mit Hilfe eines Freundes, der sich in den sozialen Medien auskennt, habe ich all diese Kommentare lesen können und den Preis sofort abgelehnt. *Blühe, Schwein, blühe!* mag den Anschein erwecken, es gehe darin in erster Linie um Schweine, die wegen eines Ausbruchs der Maul- und Klauenseuche geschlachtet wurden. Ausgehend von diesen Schweinen habe ich jedoch die Poesie als »Körper« aller Lebewesen entwickelt, menschliche Körper inbegriffen. Gleichzeitig dachte ich darüber nach, wie unsere Körper – einschließlich der Körper anderer Menschen – von unseren Blicken gefangen genommen und von Gewalt gezeichnet werden. Ich hielt mich in einem buddhistischen Tempel in Namhae auf, und jedes Mal, wenn wir – im Lotussitz ausharrend – die Worte des Mönchs vernahmen, fühlte sich mein Körper wie der eines Schweins in einem Zen-Raum an. Noch nie hatte sich mein Körper so elend gefühlt. Ich schwebte in die Luft und schaute herab auf meinen Körper. Der Körper eines Schweins, das ein Schwein frisst und behandelt wird wie ein Schwein. Ich ertappte mich dabei, wie ich Gedichte murmelte, um den Worten des Mönchs zu widersprechen oder sie zu entschuldigen, Worte, mit denen er unseren Körpern vorwarf, sich sinnlichen Gelüsten hinzugeben. Einen Körper zu haben, bedeutet, mit »Sinnen« ausgestattet zu sein und Schmerz zu empfinden. Aus der Ferne, als Schwein auf einem stummen Schweineplaneten, sah ich mich selbst auf der Erde, wie ich Schweine enthauptete, sie verspottete und dann schließlich verspeiste. Die Schweine mit ihren Sinnen und ich, ein Mensch mit eigenem Standpunkt, existierten als Gestalt gewordene Wesen in denselben Körpern, und das sogar auf verschiedenen Planeten.

Mein Gedichtband *Phantomschmerzflügel* enthält ein ziemlich langes Gedicht mit dem Titel *Gesicht des Rhythmus.*

Ich gab dem Gedicht diesen Titel, weil ich während des Schreibens das blasse Gesicht meiner Mutter sah, aufgelöst am Ende des Schmerzrhythmus – der lebendige Schmerz meines Körpers, der in Flammen stand und doch kalt war, entschwunden und doch wund und gegen meinen Willen nicht entsorgt. Anders als der Kummer war der Schmerz meines Körpers ein Rhythmus ohne Zunge. In seinem tiefsten Inneren fand sich die Realität des Rhythmus, der den Tod transzendiert und »mich« unaufhörlich in Richtung Auslöschung – die Abwesenheit meiner Mutter – drängt. Mit anderen Worten, die Besitzerin meines Schmerzes erschien mit dem Gesicht derjenigen, die meinen Körper einst zeugte und nun verschwunden war. Diese endlose Reihe von Schmerzen versank tiefer und tiefer in Intimität. Am Ende dieses Rhythmus wurden die Organe meines Körpers erschaffen, eines nach dem anderen, aber nun begegnete ich einer Lebensform, die dem Körper meiner abwesenden Mutter ähnelte und sich in meinem Körper eingenistet hatte. Vielleicht hat die Erzeugerin meines Körpers dieses »Ich« erschaffen, indem sie den Rhythmus des eigenen Körpers teilte. Einer dieser zungenlosen Rhythmen muss sich in eine Gallenblase, andere in Lungen verwandelt haben. Deshalb gab ich dem Gedicht den Titel *Gesicht des Rhythmus*. Ich glaube, dass die Poesie eine Gattung ist, die versucht, die Höhe der Musik zu erreichen, wie sie sich ausdrückt in einem leeren Gesicht, der Form der sich zum Ende hin öffnenden Lippen, und in den Schreien und Vokalen, die ohne Zunge hervorgestoßen werden. Meine Mutter war eine Zeit lang in einem Hospiz, bevor sie starb. Jedes Mal, wenn ich sie dort besuchte, fühlte ich mich, als beträte ich einen gläsernen Mixer. Mir schien, meine Mutter würde langsam ihr gesamtes Leben in diesem Mixer zermahlen, und ich spürte den Rhythmus dieses Mahlvorgangs. Die Berge und Ozeane, die sie gekannt, die Zeit, die sie verbracht, die Räume, die sie bewahrt hatte. Ich fühlte mich, als wäre ich einem

Rhythmus ausgesetzt, der alle ihre Kinder in die Mathematik der Auslöschung trieb. An dem Tag, als sie die Fähigkeit zu sprechen verlor, füllte ein Vokal den Raum, gefolgt von einem weiteren Vokal. Für mich war die Sequenz bis zum Ende dieses Vokals ein Rhythmus. Der Rhythmus, der in eine Zahl eingeht, als wäre er mit einem Wurzelzeichen versehen, der dann erlischt, um zu einem Vokal zu werden. Um dorthin zu gelangen, war der Rhythmus meiner Mutter endlos geschwommen.

Ich habe einmal ein langes Gedicht mit dem Titel *Einstiegsschacht Mensch* geschrieben. Während ich dieses Gedicht schrieb, dachte ich, dass alle Löcher der Menschen miteinander verbunden sind – unsere Hinterteile mit ihren Abwasserkanälen und Schächten, unsere Nasen und Münder mit viruslastigem Atem, unsere Augen und Ohren mit verschmutzter Luft und mit Lärm. Die Menschen in dieser Welt sind vertikal geteilt und seitlich getrennt, unter anderem aufgrund ihrer Hautfarbe und ethnischen Zugehörigkeit. Doch die Rohre unter unseren Körperöffnungen sind alle miteinander verbunden. Dazu gehören die Rohre in Hotelzimmern und die Rohre in Baracken, die Rohre in psychiatrischen Kliniken und die Rohre in Kathedralen sowie die Rückseiten asiatischer, schwarzer und weißer Menschen. Irgendwann kam ich zu der Überzeugung, dass unsere Körperöffnungen alle miteinander verbunden sind. Schließlich öffnen wir dieselben Löcher in unseren Gesichtern und unter unseren Füßen, setzen sie auf dieselben Rohre, schlicht, um weiterzuleben. Man könnte es eine Verbindung des Mangels oder eine Verbindung des Schmutzes nennen. Wenn wir gemeinsam dem Tod entgegenlaufen, so laufen wir vielleicht auf das gleiche Loch zu. Meine »Schachtmenschheit« ist gleichberechtigt verbunden durch diese Art zungenloser Löcher. Und ich dachte, dass man unsere Behausung, die Prozesse des Flusses und auch das Ungleichgewicht, das all die Formen dieser zungenlosen Löcher und Rohre umfasst, als Rhythmus beschreiben könnte.

Wenn man Prosa schreibt, nachdem man Gedichte schrieb, ist es nicht einfach, danach zur Poesie zurückzukehren. In der Poesie ist die Beziehung zwischen Dichter:in und Objekt nicht eins zu eins, sondern eine Beziehung von vielen zu vielen, und deshalb müssen, um in die und aus der 1:1-Welt zu gelangen, in welcher die eigene Sprache als so selbstverständlich angesehen wird, mehrere Raumschiffe gleichzeitig starten. Denn die Poesie unterscheidet sich von der Prosa, in der ein und dasselbe Ich mit in sich konsistenter Emotion und Logik voranschreitet. Vielleicht ist Poesie eine Gattung, die das Schreiben ablehnt. Poesie wird von jemandem verfasst, der ausgeschlossen wurde aus dem Schreiben und aus der menschlichen Zeit. Die Poesie ist das Schreiben des Zurückgewiesenen. In ihr geht es nicht einfach nur um Anspielungen, so wie auch ein Roman mehr ist als nur Fiktion. Poesie ist keine Gattung, die mit Kritiker:innen Verstecken spielt. Poesie ist eine Stimme. Sie ist eine Stimme, die sichtbar und hörbar macht, was noch nicht verbalisiert worden ist und nicht verbalisiert werden kann. In dieser Stimme hat sich die Bedeutung aufgelöst und ist verschwunden. Dies geht der Begriffsbildung voraus – wie bei einem Menschen, der noch keine Sprache erlernt hat. Die Poesie wird geschrieben, um den Lesenden nachhaltig zu verstören, der sich fragt: »Was bedeutet dieses Gedicht? Was ist deine Weltanschauung? Was deine Identität?« In der Poesie bezieht sich die Sprache der Poesie nicht auf die Eigenschaften des Objekts. Das liegt daran, dass man nicht in einer Sprache von Objekten sprechen kann. Objekte sprechen in Echos, und das tun auch die Dichter:innen. Die Stimme, die entsteht, sobald sich diese beiden Echos vermischen, ist die Sprache der Poesie. Der Körper der Dichter:innen ist ein erweiterter Körper, in den Objekte überpflanzt wurden. Die Poesie geht jedoch davon aus, dass die kognitiven Fähigkeiten eines Menschen nicht ausreichen, um einen Gegenstand vollständig zu erfassen und zu beschreiben. Das Objekt gibt Stimmen auf mehreren Ebenen wieder, wie polyphone Musik. In der Tat ist Poesie so etwas wie eine stumme Unterredung – eine Art Geräusch, zusammengesetzt aus dem Nuscheln, Murmeln und Schwanken von vielen. Wenn dies geschieht, können die Dichter:innen diese »Stimme« nicht ertragen, außer als zwiespältige, irrationale Stimme des »Affekts«. Vor allem besitzt von Frauen geschrieben Poesie, welche häufig ausgeschlossen und getötet wurde, kein autonomes Subjekt, sondern ein Aggregat verschiedener materieller und physischer Organe, ein Amalgam davon, und jene Stimme, mit Hilfe derer die Gespenster dieser Organe flüstern. Die Leser:innen treten aus dem Raum ihres Ichs heraus und gehen ein in die Leere der Bedeutung, sie betreten den perforierten Satz. Sie begeben sich in den offenen Raum der Worte, die dem Gemurmel von Glenn Gould am Klavier ähneln – so wie Gegenstände und Leben in dem Moment, in welchem sie sich in poetische Bilder verwandeln, zu Varianten des Originals werden. In jedem Augenblick eines jeden Tages sind die Stimmen der verschiedenen Varianten zu hören, und die Sprache, die sich darauf bezieht, ist zugleich eine Sprache und eine gebrochene Stimme. Sie wird zu einem Paukenschlag, der das feste Zentrum mit Abwesenheit trifft.

Wenn ich in Korea eine Lesung gebe, werde ich oft gefragt: »Warum schreiben Sie Gedichte?« und »Was bedeuten Ihre Gedichte?« Das koreanische Publikum geht, nachdem es Gedichte gehört hat, offen um mit seiner Frustration. In anderen Teilen der Welt werde ich jedoch immer wieder gefragt: »Warum gibt es in Ihren Gedichten Anklänge an den Surrealismus?« Diejenigen, die ihr Wissen über die koreanische Literatur unter Beweis stellen wollen, stellen eine spezifischere Frage: »Verglichen mit China und Japan entdeckte Ihr Korea den Surrealismus erst relativ spät, wer hat Sie also beeinflusst, surrealistische Gedichte zu schreiben?« Solche Fragen bringen mich zum Nachdenken: Wie kommt es, dass man alle unbekannten Dinge als Surrealismus bezeichnet? Auf dem Gebiet der Kunst gibt es Installationen, Medienarbeiten, unterschiedliche Ausdrucksformen, Disziplinen und Methoden, aber man bezeichnet es nicht als Surrealismus. Wenn es jedoch um Poesie geht, sagen die Leute, es sei Surrealismus, sobald sich etwas den eigenen Kriterien entzieht, anstatt das Ausdrucksmedium, die Methodik oder das Territorium poetischen Sprechens als etwas grundsätzlich anderes zu betrachten. »Wie kommt es, dass das ›sur‹** von vor 100 Jahren immer noch sauer schmeckt?« Es ergibt für mich keinen Sinn, dass mir Ausländer:innen vom Surrealismus in meiner Poesie erzählen, obwohl ich keine Lehrerin hatte, die meine Wertschätzung für Poesie förderte, kein dichterisches Vorbild, das mich beeinflusste. Ich vermute, dass sie sich selbst schmeicheln, wenn sie das Wort ›surreal‹ allem voranstellen, was ihnen fremd oder schwer verständlich erscheint, weil es nicht in einer ihnen geläufigen Sprache geschrieben ist. Als ich einmal Nagi Yoshikawas *Dada in Gyeongseong, Dada in Tokio* las, stieß ich auf eine Passage, in der beschrieben wird, wie Ko Hanyong 1924 vor dem Bahnhof von Seoul stand und eine Fahne hochhielt mit dem Schriftzug »Dadaismus«, um den japanischen Dadaisten Jun Tsuji bei seiner Ankunft in Gyeongseong (der alte Name von Seoul) willkommen zu heißen. Ich dachte daran, wie der Bahnhof von Seoul wohl vor einem Jahrhundert aussah, und musste laut lachen. Wer von den vielen Menschen, die sich an diesem Tag am Bahnhof versammelten, hätte gewusst, was Dadaismus ist? Wäre ich von einem ausländischen

** sur, frz. sauer

Surrealisten beeinflusst worden, hätte auch ich auf dem internationalen Flughafen von Incheon eine Fahne mit der Aufschrift »Surrealismus« geschwenkt. Als Antwort auf solche Fragen erkläre ich, dass keine Literatur das Leben selbst ist. Die Literatur ist ihrem Wesen nach unheimlich, poetisch/sauer*** und surreal. Noch bevor der Begriff ›Surrealismus‹ eingeführt wurde, gab es bereits Surrealismus in Korea, und zwar unter dem Namen *Sinseonsoseal* und *Yuseonsa*. Diese literarische Strömung in Korea wurde später Surrealismus genannt. Da meiner Poesie kein Platz in der literarischen Welt des Hier und Jetzt zugewiesen wurde, baue ich meinen eigenen Ort, an dem die grammatikalische Person und die zeitlichen Ebenen verschwinden, und erhebe dort die Stimme eines Gespenstes. Hier ein Beispiel aus der Dichtung von Heo Nanseolheon:

Nachdem sie tausend Jahre lang als Witwe gelebt hatte
schloss sie den Bund der Ehe mit einem Mann aus den
  Wassern des Himmels
Die nächtliche Musik aus der Luft läutet den Mond ein,
  er hängt am Rande des Daches
Die Göttin aus dem nördlichen Palast sinkt vor meine
  Füße, unsichtbar.
(Yuseonsa 37)

Heo Nanseolheons Yuseonsa-Zyklus trägt die Stimme des Surrealismus in sich. Er ist eine Art Selbsthypnose. Darin wird das »Hier« abgelehnt und im Voraus beklagt. Es wird gesagt, dass eine Frau, deren Mann noch lebt, verwitwet sei. Die Dichterin aus dem 16. Jahrhundert saß in einem dunklen Raum und schrieb Gedichte mit einer Blumenkrone auf dem Kopf und einem geöffneten Weihrauchfässchen auf dem Schreibtisch. Vielleicht sollte auch ich eine Blumenkrone

*** sauer und poetisch stellen im Koreanischen Homonyme dar: si

auf dem Kopf tragen und Weihrauch verbrennen, während ich Gedichte schreibe. Die Dichterin starb im Alter von 27 Jahren, nachdem sie sich irgendwo zwischen Himmel und Wirklichkeit platziert hatte, weil sie keinen Platz für ihre Poesie fand. In der realen Welt war sie eine Geisel des Patriarchats und des Schmerzes über den Verlust ihrer Kinder. In der Welt der Poesie versuchte sie jedoch, als einsame Unsterbliche die Freiheit zu genießen und ihre Stimme auf mittlerer Ebene lebendig zu halten. Heo Nanseolheon schrieb, sie bedauere drei Dinge: »Ich wurde in diesem Land geboren. Ich wurde als Frau geboren. Ich habe geheiratet.« Ich lebe im 21. Jahrhundert und bedauere dieselben Dinge. Die Frau aus dem 16. Jahrhundert, die gleichzeitig Traurigkeit, Einsamkeit, Verlassenheit und Misshandlung erlitt, erhebt sich jeden Tag aus ihrem Zimmer. Dann verlässt sie dieses Land, um zum Mond zu fliegen. Da sie in der Realität nirgendwo wohnen kann, richtet sie sich dort eine neue Bleibe ein. Sie durchquert mit ihrem ganzen Körper einen Ort, der nicht »dieses Land, eine Frau und eine Ehefrau« ist. Auf dem Weg dorthin nimmt ihr Körper, der bereits tot ist, die Stimmen von Geistern in sich auf – murmelnde Stimmen aus einem Leichnam, die nicht mit anderen geteilt werden können. Wir hören diese Stimmen mit unseren Augen. Wir hören sie mit unseren Körpern. Die Stimmen weisen das Territorium zurück, das ihnen durch die paternalistischen anderen aufgezwungen wird. Sie widersetzen sich vehement der Stimme der Normen. Im Alter von 27 Jahren nahm die Frau, die keine Krankheit hatte, ein Bad, zog sich um und behauptete: »Dieses Jahr entspricht dem Ergebnis von 3 mal 9. Heute hat der Frost die Lotosblumen rot gefärbt.« Dann schloss sie ihre Augen und stand nie wieder auf. Heo hinterließ ein Testament, in dem sie verfügte, alle ihre Werke müssten verbrannt werden, und ein großer Teil wurde tatsächlich von ihren Schwiegereltern den Flammen übergeben. Ihr Bruder Heo Gyun bewahrte jedoch einige ihrer Gedichte auf und veröffentlichte sie später in China. Einige Jahre danach sagte der fortschrittliche Gelehrte und Schriftsteller Pak Jiwon als Reaktion auf das chinesische Lob für Heo Nanseolheons Poesie: »Im Allgemeinen ist es nicht von Natur aus schön, wenn eine Frau Gedichte vorträgt.« Ein anderer ebenso fortschrittlicher Gelehrter, Hong Dae-yong, kommentierte: »Obwohl sie eine vollendete Dichterin war, blieb ihre Tugend weit hinter ihrer Poesie zurück.« Die großen männlichen Schriftsteller, die im 16. Jahrhundert alle Freiheiten besaßen, griffen bereitwillig jede Frau an, die auch nur die geringste Freiheit besaß. Der Wahnsinn oder die Symptome einer Frau können einen »anderen« Zustand anzeigen, der das Entstehen einer neuen Stimme ermöglicht. Wenn diese wahnsinnige Stimme, die von der Realität abweicht, einen Körper trägt, wird sie zum Surrealismus einer Dichterin im 16. Jahrhundert. Heo schrieb Gedichte in chinesischen Schriftzeichen. Vielleicht stellte ihre Muttersprache (Hangeul), die von Frauen verwendet und ihnen paradoxerweise aufgezwungen wurde, als starres System dar, das sie unterdrückte und ihr eine Reihe moralischer Prinzipien auferlegte. Diese Frau, die sie in Bezug auf ein Über-Ich [sprachlich] verkörpert/repräsentiert, ist mit den Normen des Mutterlandes und der Muttersprache verbunden, der Mond ein Ort, an dem Frauen, all die, die das gleiche Geschlecht haben, sich in Gleichheit wiederbegegnen können. Heos Poesie vermittelt das Vergnügen, das man eben dort hat, und die Entdeckung einer Stimme, die gegen das Über-Ich aufbegehrt. Diese Stimme schreit heraus, dass diese Person »nicht sie selbst« ist, dass dies nicht die richtige Art zu leben darstellt und dass dies nicht die reale Welt ist.

Es gab Tage, an denen jeder in Korea in einem Morast der Absurdität zu versinken schien. Die Trauernden strömten aus dem Schloss der Trauer und zogen durch die Straßen wie der Wind. Das Wetter blieb an allen Tagen bewölkt. Selbst in meinen Träumen stand ich unter dem grellen Licht der Zensur. Ich war Mitglied eines Redaktionsteams in einem Verlag – farblos, geruchlos, namenlos und ganz weit unten in der Hierarchie. Selbst gesetzt den Fall, jemand ohrfeigte mich, niemand würde es bemerken. Ich schluchzte unter meiner Decke, fragte mich, warum das Wetter jeden Tag verhangen war. Ich schickte meine Gedichte, die ich heimlich schrieb, an Literaturzeitschriften. Eines Tages wurde ich von einem Kriminalbeamten auf die Polizeiwache zitiert, wo er von mir die Adresse eines bestimmten Übersetzers verlangte und mich sieben Mal ohrfeigte. Wer gab ihm das Recht, mich zu beschimpfen? Mit einer Pinzette hebe ich den Raum an, in dem ich geohrfeigt wurde. Der Raum, der so hell beleuchtet war wie jener andere, in dem ich der Zensur die Bücher vorlegen musste. Der Raum, in dem niemand mit der Wimper zuckte, selbst als ich geschlagen wurde. In Dunkelheit und gedämpfter Stille schwebt oft nur dieser Raum, hell erleuchtet, zu mir herauf. In diesem Raum erhob der stämmige Mann mit Glatze und weißem Hemd seine dicke Hand und gab mir eine Ohrfeige. Damals hatte ich noch lange Haare. Als ich einen Schritt zurücktrat, streckte er die Hand aus, packte meine Bluse und ohrfeigte mich erneut. Als ich sagte: »Ich weiß es nicht«, schrie er: »Willst du mich verarschen? Ich frage, ob du mich verarschen willst?« zusammen mit anderen Schimpfwörtern. Ich hebe mich immer wieder mit einer Pinzette aus diesem Büro heraus, das kleiner ist als eine Streichholzschachtel. Dann schlucke ich mich selbst herunter. Aber auch dann murmelt es aus mir heraus. Ein paar Tage lang bin ich danach nicht zur Arbeit gegangen. Ich habe stattdessen, in kaum vernehmlicher Stimme, sieben Gedichte geschrieben – ein Gedicht für jede Ohrfeige. Diese Gedichte sind in meinem Gedichtband *Die Hölle dieses Sterns* enthalten. Ich war so erschrocken, dass ich einige Jahre brauchte, um sie zu veröffentlichen. Eines der Gedichte, das ausschließlich aus Schimpfwörtern besteht, wurde aus dem Gedichtband gestrichen. Der Kriminalbeamte war für den Verlag zuständig, für den ich arbeitete, und kam häufig vorbei, so, als ob nichts geschehen wäre. Er scherzte mit dem Chefredakteur, unterhielt sich mit ihm. Wann immer er auftauchte, ging ich auf die Toilette und blieb dort längere Zeit. Die Menschen in einer Geschichte befinden sich in der Welt dieser Geschichte. Wenn ich eine Geschichte aus der menschlichen Welt entferne, stelle ich fest, dass die Schnur so lang ist, dass ich sie um meinen Körper wickeln kann, und doch ist noch immer etwas davon übrig. Ein Geständnis führt zu endlos vielen weiteren Geständnissen. Ich zog meinen Körper heraus mit einer roten Schnur, gewickelt um eine Pinzette, verschloss die Schachtel und trampelte darauf herum. Auf diese Weise zertrat ich die Geschichte meiner Tage im Verlagshaus und hinterließ nur eine Stimme.

Die Stimme, die die Poesie durchquert, nähert sich, um uns mitzuteilen, unsere Welt, die wir fälschlicherweise für real und existent halten, sei nur eine Welt der Schatten, in der uns eine Kluft zum Verweilen angeboten wird. Die Stimme der Poesie behauptet nicht, es gäbe außerhalb einen anderen Ort. Stattdessen nähert sie sich und schreit, dass der Spalt dieses Ortes eine Welt der Abwesenheit zeigt, dass wir eine andere Welt »dazwischen« haben, und dass wir, da eine Lücke zwischen uns besteht, Bilder der Realität zurückbbauen müssen. In gleicher Weise informiert uns die Stimme der Poesie darüber, dass jedes Wort eine riesige Lücke enthält, die so ohrenbetäubend laut ist wie ein Refrain. Das Gemurmel und die Echos des Refrains besitzen in der Tat keinen eindeutigen Inhalt. Daher kennt die Stimme der Poesie keinen Meister. In Ermangelung eines Inhalts und eines Meisters schreibe ich Gedichte in Annäherung an das Nichts. Die Stimme der Poesie ist kein

Teil der Sprache. Sie ist auch kein Teil des Körpers. Sie hat keinen Namen. Sie ist nicht dialektisch. Die Stimme wird nicht gesprochen, sondern gehört. Sie wird nicht gehört, wenn man ihr nicht zuhört. Sie ist lediglich ein Echo. Ein Takt. Sie ist der Rhythmus selbst. Die Stimme der Poesie ist keine Handlung. Sie füllt keine Episode aus. Sie ist etwas, das plötzlich zu klingen beginnt, nachdem sie als Fragment an der Peripherie gelebt hat, in der Musik, im Herzen, in den Emotionen, ohne einen Ort, an dem sie sich niederlassen kann. Was sich offenbart, ist weder ein Bild noch eine Episode, sondern eine Stimme, die von der menschlichen Sprache unbehelligt bleibt. Eine Stimme kann über die erschlagene Zunge gehört werden, in den verlorengegangenen Dingen oder am Rande des Exils, das die Zunge einnimmt. Dichter:innen sind nur dann Dichter:innen, wenn sie diese Stimme hören – nur dann, wenn sie die Lücken in den Worten zwischen dem Verfassenden und dem Zuhörenden vernehmen. Wenn koreanische Leser:innen mich fragen: »Warum schreiben Sie Gedichte? Was bedeutet das alles?«, antworte ich, dass meine Stimme, da ich hier nicht leben kann, ohne zu sterben, zu einem Gespenst geworden ist, ein Gespenst erschuf, das immer wieder aufs Neue entsteht. Ich erkläre, dass Poesie der Tod ist und dass die Stimme des Todes im Plural spricht. Wenn mich Menschen außerhalb Koreas fragen, warum ich Surrealistin bin, bitte ich sie, mich nicht so zu nennen, weil das bedeuten würde, dass die meisten Gedichte, die in einer bestimmten Epoche und von der Person eines bestimmten Geschlechts geschrieben wurden, ebenfalls als surrealistisch bezeichnet werden müssten. Ich antworte, das Spukhaus meiner Poesie sei lediglich ein leeres Haus, das einzig von einer Stimme bewohnt wird. In diesem löchrigen Haus »macht meine Poesie Poesie«, und durch die Poesie »mache ich dich«. Ich erzähle ihnen, dass ich diesen leeren Raum mit einem großen Trommelstock schlage wie die Prinzessin von Nakrang (die nach der koreanischen Legende die mystische Trommel zerbricht, die vor einer fremden Invasion warnt, damit Prinz Hodong von Goguryeo während der Herrschaft von Daemusin (32 n. Chr.) in das Königreich Nakrang eindringen kann) und ich mich bemühe, das weibliche Vergnügen als eine andere Form der Verletzung anzubieten, die den Vater entthront. Ich antworte, dass die Luft vibriert und mitschwingt mit meiner Stimme und dass der Wind heult. Die Ausführung meiner Stimme als Dichterin findet in den Leerstellen der Muttersprache statt. Und wenn meine weiblichen und poetischen Sehnsüchte in den Leerstellen der Muttersprache erfüllt sind, kann ich endlich ein Gedicht entfalten.

김혜순 (1955년 경북 울진 출생) 은 대한민국을 대표하는 시인이다. 1970년대 후반부터 지금에 이르기까지 다수의 시를 발표하였다. 김수영 문학상 (1997), 삼성호암상 (2022) 등을 수상했으며 최돈미 시인의 영문 번역을 통해 미국에서도 명성을 누리고 있다. 시집 '죽음의 자서' (*Autobiography of Death*, New Directions Publishing, 2018) 으로 2019 년 그리핀 시문학상 (The Griffin Poetry Prize) 수상자로 선정되었다. 시선집 '구름성의 여자' (*Die Frau im Wolkenschloss*, Pendragon, 2002) 의 독일어판(김영옥 번역)이 출간되었다.

Kym Hyesoon, born in 1955 in Uljin, Kyŏngsangbuk-do, is South Korea's most important poet. She has been publishing poetry since the late 1970s. In the meantime, she has produced an extensive body of work, for which she was awarded the prestigious Kim Su-yŏng Literature Prize in 1997 and the Ho Am Prize in 2022. In the USA, she gained greater fame through translations of the poet Don Mee Choi. The book "Autobiography of Death" (New Directions Publishing 2018) won the 2019 Griffin Poetry Prize. In German, the volume "Die Frau im Wolkenschloss" (Pendragon 2002, translation: Kim Young-Ok) is available.

Kym Hyesoon, geboren 1955 in Uljin, Kyŏngsangbuk-do, ist die bedeutendste Dichterin Südkoreas. Seit Ende der 70er Jahre veröffentlicht sie Gedichte. Mittlerweile liegt ein umfangreiches Werk vor, für das Sie 1997 mit dem renommierten Kim-Su-yŏng-Literaturpreis und 2022 mit dem Ho-Am-Preis ausgezeichnet wurde. In den USA erlangte sie größere Bekanntheit durch die Übersetzungen der Dichterin Don Mee Choi. Das Buch *Autobiography of Death* (New Directions Publishing 2018) erhielt 2019 den Griffin Poetry Prize. In deutscher Sprache liegt der Band *Die Frau im Wolkenschloss* (Pendragon 2002, Übersetzung: Kim Young-Ok) vor.

Bibliografische Information der Deutschen Nationalbibliothek
Die Deutsche Nationalbibliothek verzeichnet diese Publikation in der Deutschen Nationalbibliografie; detaillierte bibliografische Daten sind im Internet über http://dnb.d-nb.de abrufbar.

www.wallstein-verlag.de
Vom Verlag gesetzt aus der Stempel Garamond
Einbandkonzept: studio stg, Berlin
Druck & Verarbeitung: Hubert & Co, Göttingen

ISBN 978-3-8353-5397-8